Mel Bay Presents

Mastering the Bass

A COMPREHENSIVE METHOD FOR ELECTRIC AND UPRIGHT BASS

By Bruce Gertz

BOOK 1

COVER AND ALL OTHER PHOTOS BY GILSTEIN PHOTOGRAPHY

CD CONTENTS

CD I

1	Tuning Note A (220) [:19]
2	Note Values, Note and Rest Values [:26]
3	Open A, Open E [1:39]
4	Repeat Brackets [:47]
5	Open Strings [1:41]
6	Open String Rhythm, Downbeat, Up Beat [1:35]
7	Adjacent G & D [1:27]
8	Adjacent D & A, A & E [2:01]
9	Dotted Note Values 4/4 [:29]
10	Dotted Note Values, Other Time Signatures [:52]
11	Waltz, Rock [1:28]
12	The Tie [:25]
13	G & D Ex.1-6 [1:43]
14	G & D Similar Rhythms [:59]
15	Triplets and 9/8 [:15]
16	Duration [:38]
17	Skipping Strings [1:49]
18	Reggae, On/Off, Triplets, Bolero [2:01]
19	Rock & Roll, Motown, 12/8 [2:11]
20	1st & 2nd Endings, Shuffle, Funk [1:17]
21	Minor Blues [1:34]
22	Sixteenths [1:36]
23	Right Hand Exercises 1-6 [1:58]
24	Right Hand Exercises 7-13 [1:28]
25	Syncopations [1:27]
26	Interval Piece [:38]
27	Grooves with 4ths and 5ths [:45]
28	First Position E String Exercises 1-7 [2:19]
29	First Position E String Exercises 8-12 [2:01]
30	First Position E String Exercises 13-18 [1:32]
31	First Position A String Exercises 1-6 [1:15]

32	First Position A String Exercises 7-14 [1:45]
33	A Major (E & A) [1:08]
34	Walking Blues C & F [1:52]
35	First Position D String Exercises 1-6 [1:12]
36	First Position D String Exercises 7-13 [1:34]
37	Walking Blues F & Bb [1:55]
38	Crossing strings A, E A, D [1:36]
39	First Position G String Exercises 1-6 [1:03]
40	First Position G String Exercises 7-13 [2:04]
41	Enharms Way [:36]
42	Walking Blues Bb & Eb [1:53]
43	Tie Exercises [2:05]
44	Never Say Never [1:07]
45	Drunken Sailor [:27]
46	Question and Answer [:34]
47	Battle of Jericho [1:09]
48	Funk Blues (G) [1:00]
49	Never Been Better [2:22]
50	Duet, God Bless America [:51]
51	Duet, My Bonnie Lies Over The Ocean [:49]
52	Musical Ears [:17]
53	Ear Training Rhythm Exercise #1 [:35]
54	Ear Training Rhythm Exercise #2 [:24]
55	Ear Training, Harmonic/Rhythmic Dictation [:48]

CD 2

1	Tuning Note A (220) [:19]
2	Pentatonic Piece [:58]
3	Pentatonic Bass Lines [:43]
4	Variations on a Funky Theme [:37]
5	Rhythmic Notation/Reading Roots [1:49]
6	Roots & Fifths C [:37]

7	Roots & Fifths, Various Keys [:51]
8	Bb Blues/Roots, Roots & Fifths [:53]
9	Blues, Chords Only [:45]
10	Reading Basic Chord Charts, Walk & Two Feel [2:03]
11	Roots, Fifths & Octaves [:43]
12	Walk with Roots, Fifths & Octaves [:14]
13	A minor, Bossa Nova [1:10]
14	6/8 Latin [2:21]
15	Grooves/Vamps with Roots & Fifths [1:31]
16	Grooves/Vamps 3/4, 5/4 and More [1:31]
17	Major Scales 1st Position, Bass Guitar [:46]
18	Minor Scales 1st Position, Bass Guitar [1:25]
19	Minor Scales, Diminished Scales [:50]
20	Diminished Scales & Modes [:37]
21	Double Stops, Check Points for Intonation [:22]
22	1st Position Modes E Mixolydian-Bb Phrygian [1:42]
23	1st Position Modes F# Phrygian-Bb Chromatic [1:42]
24	1st Position Modes Gb Chromatic-G#7 Altered [:54]
25	1st Position Chord Arpeggios from Open E [2:28]
26	1st Position Chord Arpeggios from F [2:29]
27	1st Position Chord Arpeggios from F# [2:29]
28	1st Position Chord Arpeggios from G [2:29]
29	1st Position Chord Arpeggios from Ab [2:30]
30	1st Position Chord Arpeggios from A [2:29]
31	1st Position Chord Arpeggios from Bb [2:30]
32	1st Position Chord Arpeggios from Bb (Fast) [2:29]
33	1st Position Chord Arpeggios from B [2:29]
34	1st Position Chord Arpeggios from C [2:29]
35	1st Position Chord Arpeggios from C# [2:29]
36	1st Position Chord Arpeggios from D (Slow/Fast) [2:30]
37	1st Position Chord Arpeggios from Eb [2:33]

The play-along CD is programmed to help you learn to read and hear music. The CD tracks often have multiple examples to read along with. Either the beat continues through an entire page or a new count off will occur. Keep moving and in a reasonably short time you will begin reading music or improve your current ability. Upright and fretless bassists can improve their intonation by matching pitch with the fretted bass guitar or chords from the keyboard on the tracks.

With the exception of a few tracks the bass is only in the left speaker on your stereo. Panning the balance you may eliminate the bass or focus on the recorded bass.

Special thanks to Peter Moutis for supplying live drums on the following tracks: CD-1 tracks 20, 28-38, 40-42, CD-2 tracks 5-14. And to my family, Roberta, Ruby, Eva and parents, Minnie and Ray Gertz for love and support. For more information on Bruce Gertz visit www.brucegertz.com.

Visit us on the Web at www.melbay.com — E-mail us at email@melbay.com

1 2 3 4 5 6 7 8 9 0

Table of Contents

Coming in Book 2 of *Mastering the Bass!*

Position Studies, Shifting between positions
Learning to look ahead and improve your reading!
Triad and Scale studies, pieces, solos, bass parts (all styles)
Theory, Diatonic Harmony, minor scales, Interval Studies, Interpreting chord symbols
Basic Improvisation, Bass lines, Grooves, Ear Training, Rhythm and Pitch Exercises, Duets

What does it mean to be a Bassist?

Being a bassist means much more than carrying large instruments and heavy equipment. The job is much more demanding than that. It involves a deep understanding of rhythm, harmony and melody along with a willingness to be supportive to other instrumentalists. Bass is usually the foundation of the music in which it is employed. In fact the bass and melody are referred to as the primary diaphony, (first two voices of the music). They are the top and bottom of the music. For this and other reasons the bass is ultimately important and very much relied upon. A strong, sensitive bass player is always in demand.

Although the bass is a beautiful solo instrument it is heard more often in its supportive, foundational role. One reason that a bass solo is special is that it happens less frequently than horn, string, piano/keyboard or other solos. On a personal level it is common for us to want to be in the spotlight at times and this can present a challenge to our willingness to be supportive. Personality is a strong factor in choosing a band and sometimes a less flashy player will get a job because they have the right attitude.

Patience can help strengthen personal relationships and musical ones. The ability to blend tastefully in a musical group is very much like a social skill. One must listen as well as speak. Since the inception of the bass it has evolved and become more of a solo instrument with many styles of performers. At the same time accompaniment skills have also evolved and are sometimes complex. We must be prepared as musicians to follow our own path and let the music lead us.

A bassist with a good attitude, solid time keeping skills (groove vocabulary), along with a warm tone, correct harmony (right notes), good intonation (playing in tune) will always be in demand.

It is important to distinguish between solo (melody) playing and comping (rhythm, harmony, accompaniment) playing. One can be a great groove player and then turn out a killer solo at the appropriate time. The following two principles should be followed.
1. Always strive to make the group and individual lead players sound the very best with your support.
2. When playing a solo or a fill always try to be as tasteful as possible.

To Become a Master

To become a master requires a total devotion to learning that craft. A master is someone who has strong, consistent skills and executes them perfectly with only the effort required to do so. This mastery requires experience and practice. When the question is asked, "how much should I practice?" the correct answer is, "until you have mastered what you're working on."

This book is designed to give the student a thorough, gradual study of obtainable musical goals including a strong rhythmic foundation upon which bass playing must be built. That is the reason for the great number of short repeated grooves and vamps as well as a myriad of open string and first position studies. The intention is not to limit the player to the low positions but to insure the mastery of the bass register as well as all other registers of the instrument and introduce a wide range of musical examples. Some music requires an entire lifetime of practice. Being a Master does not mean that the Master need not practice anymore. One should always try to improve and learn new music. This is the example true Masters set for others to follow.

When a musical example, (simple or difficult), is mastered by a student, there is a tremendous sense of satisfaction and accomplishment. With each mastered piece comes more fulfillment. Good luck, work hard and have fun mastering the bass!

Setting Goals

We all have dreams of how we would like to be able to perform. These visions can be realized gradually through practice and experience. Once it is clear what we need to achieve in order to perform at the desired level, goals can be set to lead us to our best playing experiences and make the dreams a reality. Here is a check list of goals broken down into levels beginning with the ultimate goal.

"Freedom of Expression Through Musical Mastery"

Although the ultimate goal may seem unattainable at first taking the right steps will help you reach it. The following are subsequent goals.

- **Being able to play what you hear.**
- **Hearing and understanding a wide range of music.**
- **Creating interesting parts on your instrument which function well and contribute to a good group sound.**
- **Interpreting styles of music with the correct feeling and articulation.**
- **Playing solid grooves with momentum.**
- **Reading chord charts with notes, rhythms and form combined.**
- **Improvising.**
- **Reading rhythms.**
- **Reading chord changes.**
- **Reading notes.**
- **Picking out parts by ear from recordings and playing them perfectly.**
- **Being able to play any arpeggio or scale. (instrumental familiarity)**
- **Singing tonality (major, minor scales and arpeggios), in time.**
- **Hearing tonality and basic rhythm.**

Now that we have a list of goals here is a practice routine to follow which should bring you to them with a bit of patience and a good deal of diligence.

How to Practice

When starting out on an instrument adhering to a regular practice routine (4-7 times a week, 8-56 hours per week) will certainly bring results. Of course the more, valuable time you put in, the more musical ability you will have. You can/should also practice away from your instrument, singing and visualizing what fingerings and articulation would fit the music you sing. Rhythmic, harmonic and melodic ear training are also necessary to practice. After you've established solid technique, practicing remains essential to grow as a musician. When our time becomes limited practice time can be adjusted to fit in the schedule. With limited time it is best to focus on a particular goal. This way you won't be overwhelmed with a mountain of material to master. Below is a regular practice routine you may follow. Although warm up exercises are always best to do first, the rest of the items can be in different orders and if time is limited focus may be placed in an area that you want to improve.

Practice Routine

Step 1. Technique (playing in tune with good time and feeling).
Warm up with long even tones on scales, arpeggios and exercises. Be sure to include keys that you are less familiar with. Don't limit yourself to the key of C. Play each exercise slow and even first then build up tempo gradually. Use time references such as metronomes, drum machines, play-along CD's etc. Also practice exercises without these references maintaining the best time/rhythm possible. (developing your internal metronome). Sing all your exercises.

Step 2. Reading (pitch, rhythm, dynamics, phrasing and articulation), involves many aspects which at first may need to be broken down. To develop reading pitch you may ignore the rhythm and play each note 4-8 times each (see "Learning to Read"). The same goes for rhythm; ignore the pitch and work out the subdivisions. When you are ready put the two together eventually add the details (dynamics, phrasing etc.) Reading with play-alongs can help by allowing you to hear what the music should sound like however keep reading. Once you have learned a piece it is no longer fresh reading material. It is in your memory. Try to have fresh, unfamiliar material to practice reading. Don't stop. Keep looking forward and playing the music. If you make mistakes don't stop to fix them. Make mental notes where things went wrong. You can read the whole piece again and again with less mistakes each time. Train yourself to look ahead and not stop.

Step 3. Piece(s), to perfect are an important part of practicing which address a number of goals. When learning a piece of music it helps to hear it if possible. Try singing the phrases to yourself and visualizing how to play them. Read the piece and learn the phrases. If necessary isolate the phrases and work on them until they're strong and then you may put the phrases together and work on continuity. Dynamics, articulation, bowings, positions, fingerings and emotion are all elements of performing a piece of music. Interpretation is an extremely important part of playing pieces, particularly in classical music. Some pieces require a lifetime of devotion. In those cases it is important to realize the growth process involved with the piece and not get carried away with frustration if you lose patience while working on such a piece. Many pieces are not lifetime achievements and can be mastered in time with diligent practice. When a piece is under your fingers and you are singing on your instrument it is a feeling of elation.

Step 4. Improvisation and Ear Training are closely related and can be very enjoyable practice. The most valuable lesson in improvisation is listening and practicing playing what you hear. Ultimately you want to hear creatively and play that music. Practice singing/playing melodies and grooves, with/without play-alongs. Work with and without chord changes. Learn standard tunes (melody, chord changes, bass lines, etc.), play with friends, radio, TV, drum machines, solo, etc. Listen to recordings and figure out parts (transcribe), and learn to play them. Write lines (melodic, walking, rhythmic, funk, odd meter, etc.) and learn to play them. Build a vocabulary from which you can draw and create new ideas.

INTRO TO BASICS

Fingering Hand

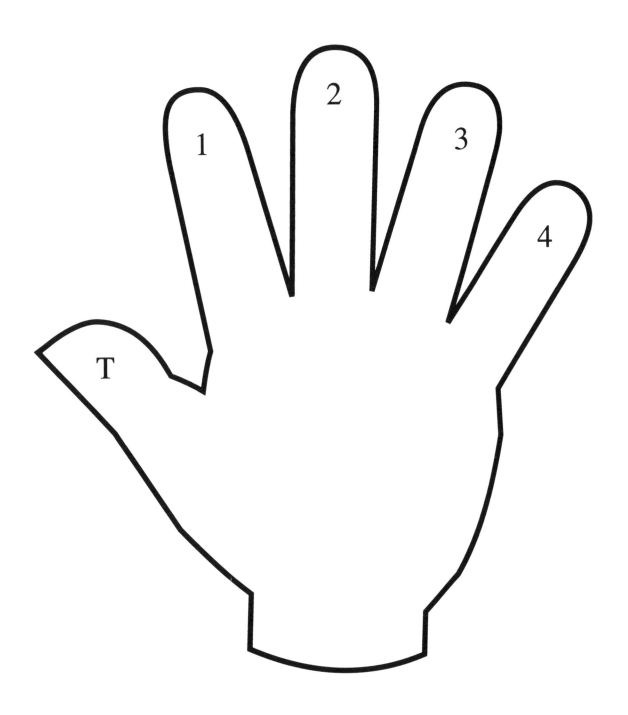

Parts of the Bass Guitar

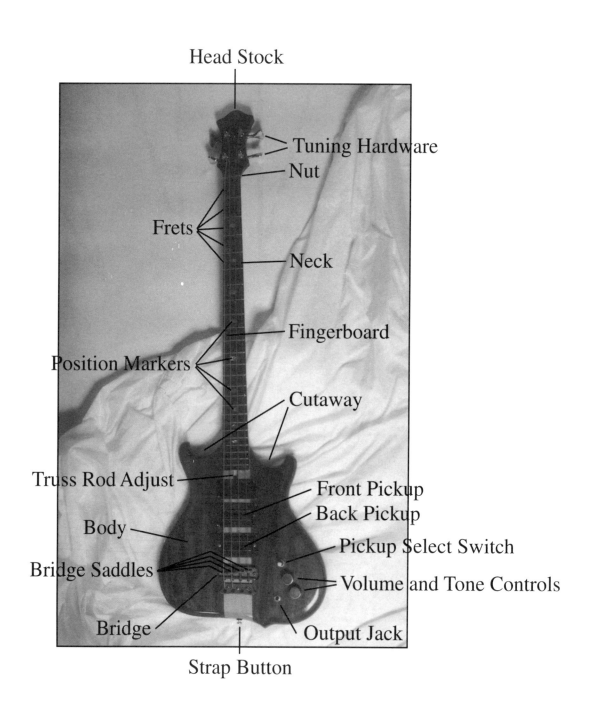

Head Stock

Tuning Hardware

Nut

Frets

Neck

Fingerboard

Position Markers

Cutaway

Truss Rod Adjust

Front Pickup

Back Pickup

Body

Pickup Select Switch

Bridge Saddles

Volume and Tone Controls

Bridge

Output Jack

Strap Button

Parts of the Upright Double Bass

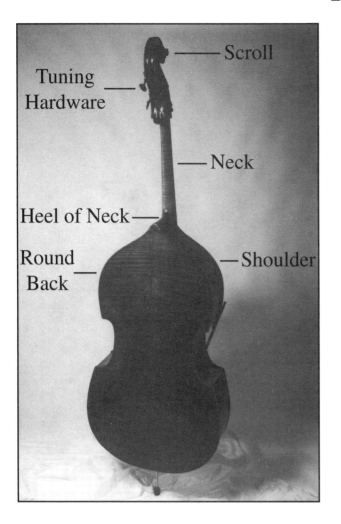

Scroll

Tuning Hardware

Neck

Heel of Neck

Round Back

Shoulder

The bass shown is a typical 3/4 size roundback. Some basses have flat backs with internal rib supports. Basses are made with spruce tops, maple back, sides and neck. The fingerboard and tailpiece may be ebony or rosewood. Bridges are a hard maple wood.

Some basses are plywood (laminated) with maple necks and fingerboards. There are also hybrid instruments of plywood, spruce, rosewood, ebony, maple, mahogany in various combinations. Most necks are hard maple.

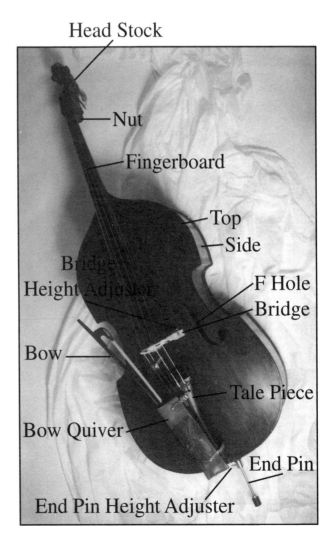

Head Stock

Nut

Fingerboard

Top

Side

Bridge Height Adjuster

F Hole

Bridge

Bow

Tale Piece

Bow Quiver

End Pin

End Pin Height Adjuster

Standing With the Bass Guitar (Electric)

Maintaining good posture and remaining relaxed will help avoid shoulder, neck and back pain or injury. Keep the wrists relaxed and not too bent. Always keep both hands as close to the notes as possible. "Play into the instrument."

Sitting With the Bass Guitar (Electric)

Sit up straight and relaxed. If not using a strap the body will rest on the thigh. As previously mentioned, do not over bend the wrists and play into the instrument.

Standing Pizzicatto (Plucking)

Maintain good posture. Feet are shoulder length apart and weight centered. Stay relaxed.

End pin height adjustment should be fixed so the nut is in line with the eye brow of the player when standing straight. This will ensure the correct positions of the right and left hands relative to the string length, enabling the best placement for both attack and reaching all the notes comfortably.

Standing at ease, expressing positive attitude to other band members and audience.

Contemplating next piece of music before playing.

Sitting (Upright Bass) Pizzicatto

Maintain good posture in your back, neck and shoulders

Before

Here a note is played on the A string.

After plucking the A string the plucking finger comes to rest on the lower string.

After

Right Hand Pizzicatto (Plucking)

1) Typical 60° pizzicatto. Fingers at 60 degree angle to strings. Let the string roll out from the finger. Other unplayed strings are damped by the side of the index finger.

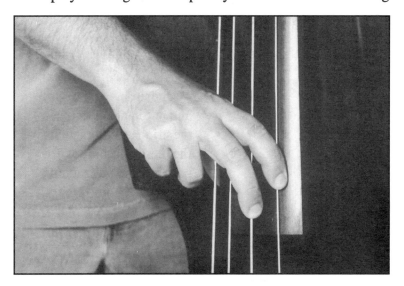

2) Typical 30° pizzicatto. Some players hold the finger at less of an angle to the strings. Less flesh comes in contact with the string and it creates a different sound. Experiment.

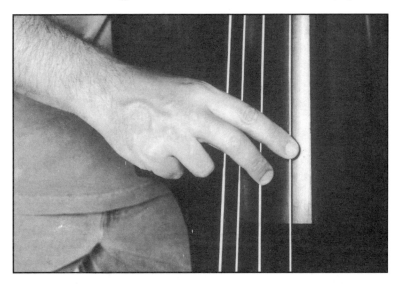

Power Pizz. Double (2) finger attack is good for heavy playing at different tempos.

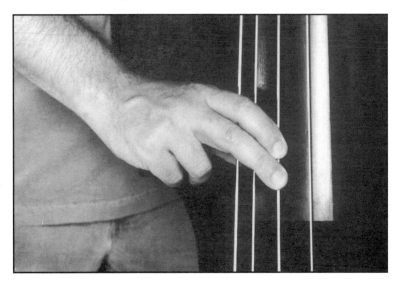

Thumb Placement, Left Hand (Upright Bass)

The thumb should be placed somewhere between the first and second finger in the middle or crest of the back of the neck to provide leverage to the fingering hand. Only use the pressure needed to produce a solid tone. Don't squeeze the neck tightly.

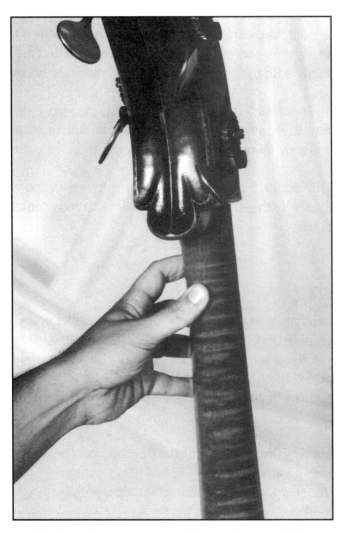

Behind and in between the first and second finger

Behind the first finger.

Right Hand/Left Hand/Damping

The right hand or attack hand should be positioned in a way which is most efficient for plucking. There are different approaches to playing electric and acoustic bass. First and most popular are the first two fingers of the right hand in an alternating pattern. You can begin the alternating with the first or second finger and should practice both. Try to play as evenly with two fingers as you can with the same finger. Time signatures and phrasing will often dictate the method. There is no set way and most players find a comfortable approach however the music will help determine how we can achieve the needed result. Dynamics will require a hard medium or soft attack and articulations may call for less attacks with slurs, pull-offs or hammer-ons. In a funk style players often slap the strings against the finger board with their thumb. Another style is tapping the notes directly with the fingers on the fingerboard. Others use a guitar pick and some players do it all.

Begin by learning the fingerstyle which is the most common one. With the exception of using fingers or a pick all other techniques are specialties and won't be used as often. Remember that it is important to build a strong foundation. Acoustic bass players should practice everything with a bow as well as pizzicato to build strong technique.

The right wrist should not be bent too much because it stretches the tendons and this can lead to physical problems such as tendinitis. The manner in which the right hand falls naturally to the strings of the acoustic is a good example to follow when approaching the electric bass strings. See figures.

Damping

Damping or keeping unwanted notes from ringing is extremely important. The pure tone of individual notes or simple chords projects clearly when no interference exists. Keeping the bass quiet is an art in itself. One must use both hands employing the unused fingers to dampen the strings. Another reason is readiness. If your fingers are flying away from the instrument it requires more time to get back for the next passage. Each situation requires the appropriate damping. Generally it seems awkward at first but comes naturally as your musicianship develops. See figures.

The left hand should remain relaxed as it stays as close to the strings as possible with the fingers evenly positioned enabling the easiest access to the notes on the finger board, (see photo).

On fretted bass put your fingers between the frets close to the sharp side of the note. On fretless put your fingers directly where the fret would be. Usually there are position markers on the side of the neck.

On upright bass the accuracy of pitch (intonation) is dependent strictly upon the left hand position, measuring the distance between notes with the fingers of your left hand. This is a great mental discipline. Also maintaining a good hand position is crucial to playing in tune.

Left Hand Thumb Placement (Electric Bass)

Most often the left thumb is best placed behind the first or second finger or somewhere in between at the crest of the back of the neck. For some passages the thumb may be moved around and employed in different ways.

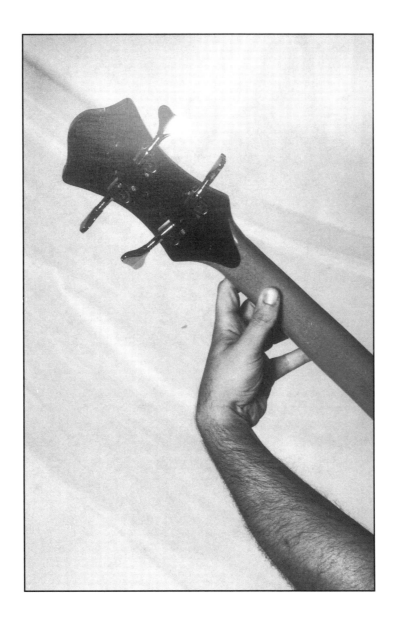

Depending on the passage you are playing it may be more comfortable to have your thumb behind your index finger.

Damping With the Right Hand (Electric, Bass Guitar)

Except for the notes you are playing the bass must be quiet. With the fingers not being used to play notes keep the rest of the bass quiet by damping or covering the strings.

Muting With All Four Fingers (Right hand)

Damping With Both Hands

The first finger of the left hand is keeping the D and A strings quiet. The right hand thumb is resting on E and A strings while the index finger is playing the G string. The only note ringing should be C on the G string.

By slightly raising the elbow of the plucking arm one reduces the angle and lessons the stretching of the tendons. (See previous page)

Another cause of injury is the motion of the left hand, (fingering hand), away from the neck of the instrument. (See Bad Habits)

Generally when using the third or fourth finger, (left hand), for notes on the neck keep the first and second fingers down on the string(s) as well. For the most part the first and second fingers are strong enough on their own. A good rule is to "Always play into the instrument, (bass), and avoid playing away, (outward motion). This keeps you close to the notes on the neck and will contribute to speed and accuracy. If your fingers are too far away from the instrument it will cost you time and energy to get back to play the notes. If you're already there the time and energy needed are minimized and you'll be that much closer to mastery. (See Good Technique and Bad Habits)

Good Technique for the Left Hand (Upright Bass)

When playing notes with the fourth (pinky) finger, let the other fingers lay against the fingerboard gently to add support to the little finger.

Good Technique (Upright Bass)

When playing note (A♭) on the G string with the index finger keep the other 3 fingers close to the fingerboard.

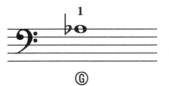

Here is a double stop (2 notes together), under the index finger. The other fingers rest against the fingerboard, out of the way allowing the G string to ring.

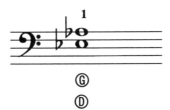

Bad Habits, Things to Avoid

Avoid fingers flying away from the fingerboard. This is counterproductive and could cause injury.

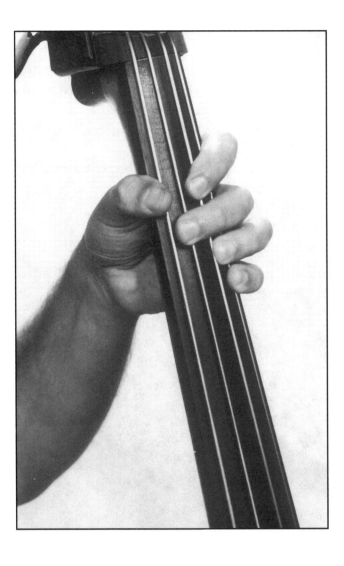

Avoid clenching the neck.

Avoid having the middle fingers high off the neck while the two outer fingers are down. This is a very dangerous habit and causes wrist and tendon problems.

Fingerstyle
Right Hand (Attack) Electric, Tone Production

The string is pulled slightly when the plucking finger (s) is pressed against the string and drawn inward toward the palm allowing the string to roll off the tip of the finger.

Experiment with different amounts of pressure for dynamics (loud, soft). Strive for even sound from one attack to the next.

String tension is greater near the bridge and a crisp sound (brighter tone) can be accomplished plucking there. Closer to the fingerboard the sound is more mellow (deeper, darker). However, the resound of the string is slower at that point. Most bassists play somewhere between these points depending on the desired tone.

The wrist of the plucking hand should not be bent much greater than 45°.

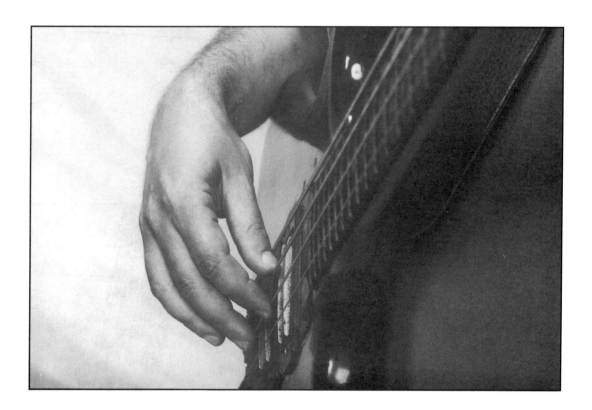

Fingerstyle, Bass Guitar
Thumb Placement, Plucking Hand

To minimize the reach to the D and A strings rest the thumb on the E string. This will also damp the E string.

To minimize reaching the D and G strings rest the thumb on the A string and the side of the thumb on the E string.

Using a Pick or Plecktrum

Hold the pick between the thumb and bent index finger. Apply pressure to the string and snap the pick across striving for an even sound with down and up strokes.

Down stroke to G string

Up stroke to G string

Left Arm Almost Perpendicular to the Neck

Elbow raised away from the body of the bass.

 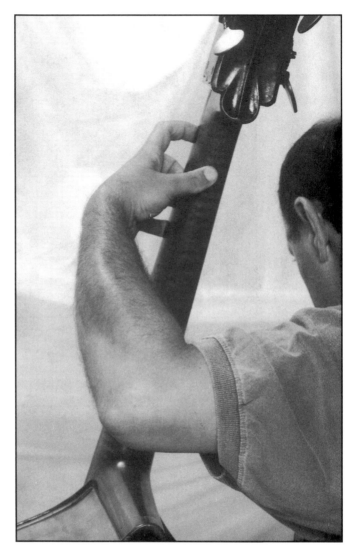

Bow Grip/French Style

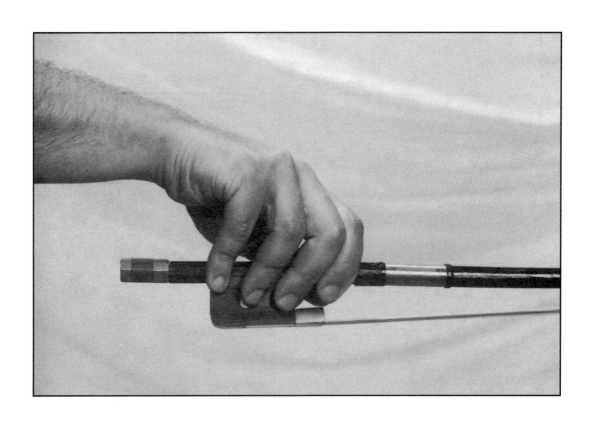

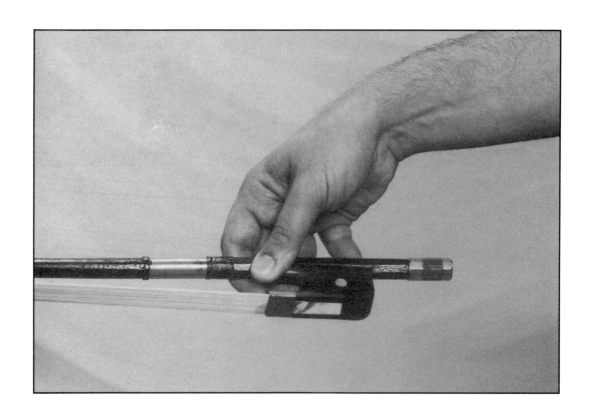

Bow Grip/German Style

Bow Placement, Drawing the Bow, Tone Production

Place the hair of the bow at the wide end (frog) on the string. With enough rosin the bow should grab the string as you draw it toward you with a little pressure to get it vibrating.-------- If you look at the string while bowing it you'll see it rotating. It may require an extra pop of pressure to start the sound but once it's rolling less pressure is needed to maintain sound. The tone is brighter near the bridge and darker near the fingerboard.

French

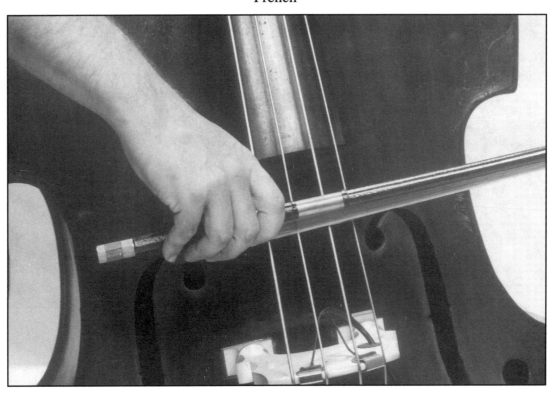

German

Standing ARCO (Bowing) Position

Practice all the exercises in this book arco, (with the bow) as well as pizzicato, (with the fingers). This will help you develop good intonation and technique. For now just play everything in a back and forth motion down bow-up bow. Later in training when you've mastered measuring how much bow to use for note values we can address other bowings.

<table>
<tr><td>⌐¬</td><td>∨</td></tr>
<tr><td>Down Bow</td><td>Up Bow</td></tr>
</table>

Down Bow

Draw the bow toward you. Placement of bow hair should be between the bridge and the end of the fingerboard for normal playing at moderate to loud volume levels.

Up Bow

Pushing the bow with the elbow only slightly bent. The bow should be perpendicular to the strings for both down and up bows.

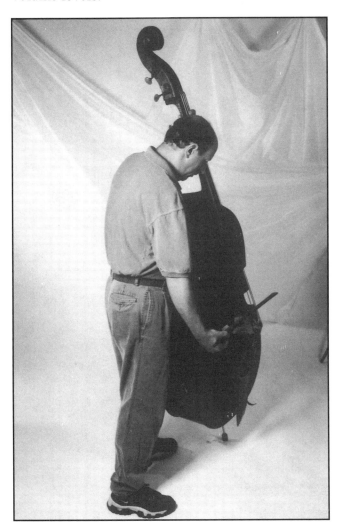

Bow Arm

Good, wrist bent, elbow almost straight.

Yes

Bad, right elbow bent too much and wrist not bent enough. (This is called "sawing wood" as a joke.)

No

Tuning the Bass

The bass is normally tuned in perfect fourths E, A, D, G from low to high.

Here are some common methods of tuning.

Upright bass players should tune with the bow.

1. Match the open strings to the same notes on a piano or keyboard. Listen for beats or vibrations that indicate you're out of tune. When there are no waves beating against each other and you hear a flat line, it's in tune. Holding an A 440 pitch fork near the pickup or against the bridge on the upright bass is also good.

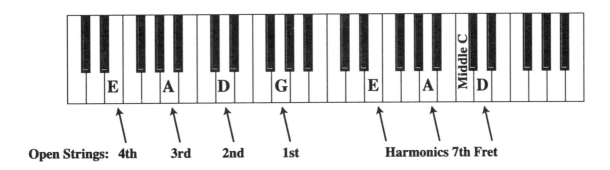

2. Harmonics on the 7th fret or a perfect 5th above the open string are a common method used by classical players. Touching the string at the fret or note without depressing it will yeild the harmonic which is one octave and a perfect 5th above the open string.

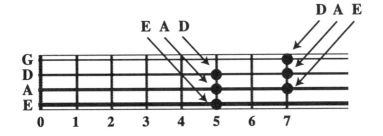

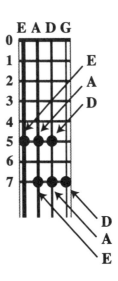

33

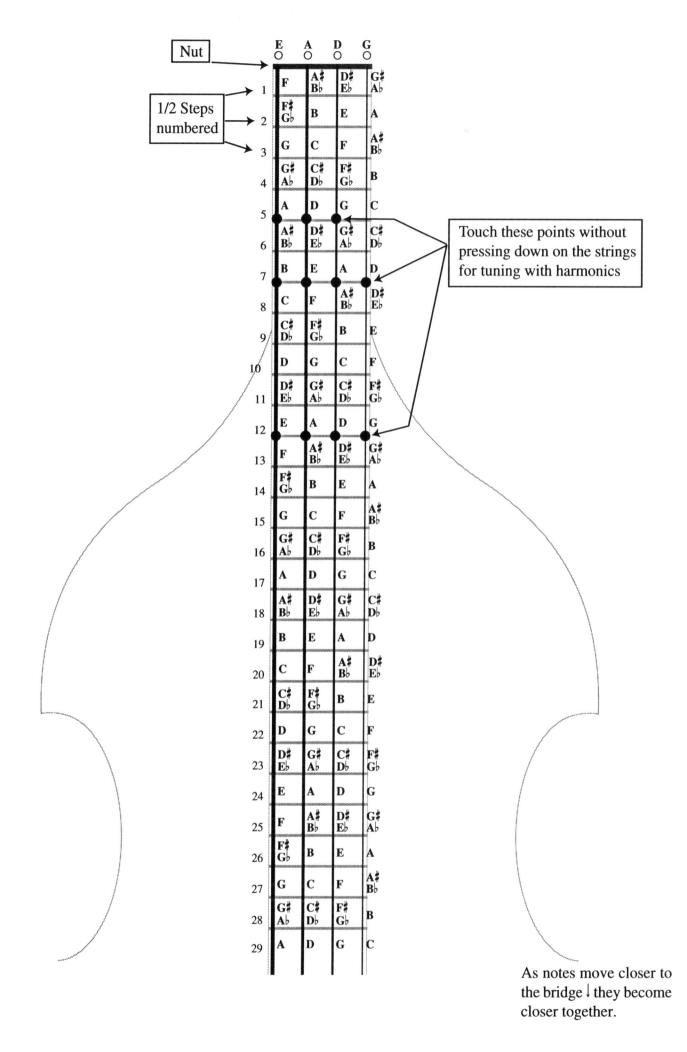

Nut

1/2 Steps numbered

Touch these points without pressing down on the strings for tuning with harmonics

As notes move closer to the bridge ↓ they become closer together.

34

Tuning With Harmonics, Use Bow

Most classical and jazz bassists tune with harmonics because the frequency of the higher pitch is much easier to hear accurately than the low open strings. Approximately at the crook of the neck the following notes D, A, E, B when touched, (not pressed down) will yield an octave higher, the same notes.

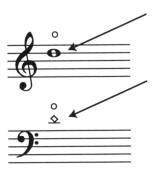

Written pitch

A diamond notehead is a note that is touched but not pressed down.
A small circle (°) above a note usually indicates a harmonic. The position of these harmonics is a perfect fifth above the open string.

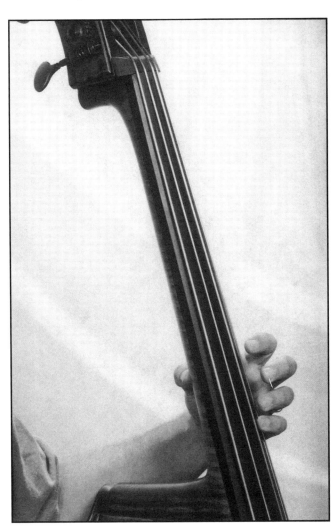

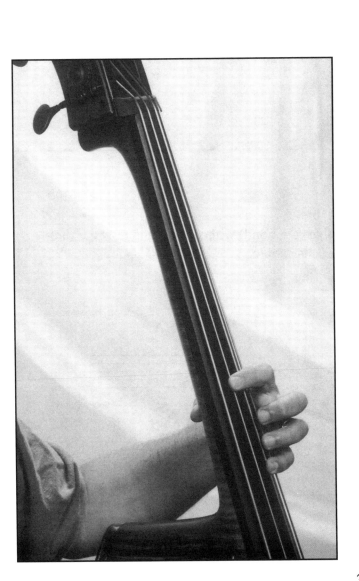

Here under the fourth finger on the D string is the note A. A matching A exists under the first finger on the A string. Other matching notes in the same position are the harmonics D on the D string and E on the E string. The equivalent position on electric bass is the seventh fret harmonics D, A, E and B with matching harmonics D, A and E at the fifth fret.

Tuning With Harmonics at the 7th Fret

Touching the string and plucking it at the indicated note (diamond) without pressing down to the fingerboard gives you a harmonic.

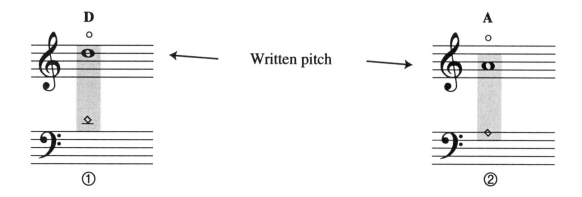

Matching Harmonics at the 5th and 7th Frets

Across two adjacent strings as in the figure below will result in a perfect unison (same note)
if the bass is in tune. (no beats or vibrations)

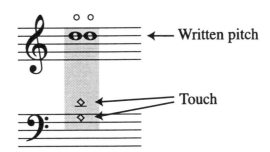

Tuning the Bass (Continued)

After tuning the 7th fret harmonic to the piano find a matching pitch at the 5th fret or half step on the adjacent string below, (D on the G string 7th fret and D on the D string, 5th fret). Play the harmonic, D on the G string, then the harmonic, D on the D string and tune the D string until the beats disappear.

3. Match the open strings to an electronic tuner. Certain kinds handle low frequencies better than others. This method is fool proof but does not force you to use your ears.

4. Matching the 5th fret of each string to the open string above is a popular method for guitar however on bass the frequency is quite low to hear accurately.

5. Play the open G string and the 12th fret harmonic on the D string. Listen for a perfect 5th. Repeat the same procedure on the D and A strings and finally A and E strings.

6. Tune to A 220 from CD 1, track 1. CD 1 Track #1

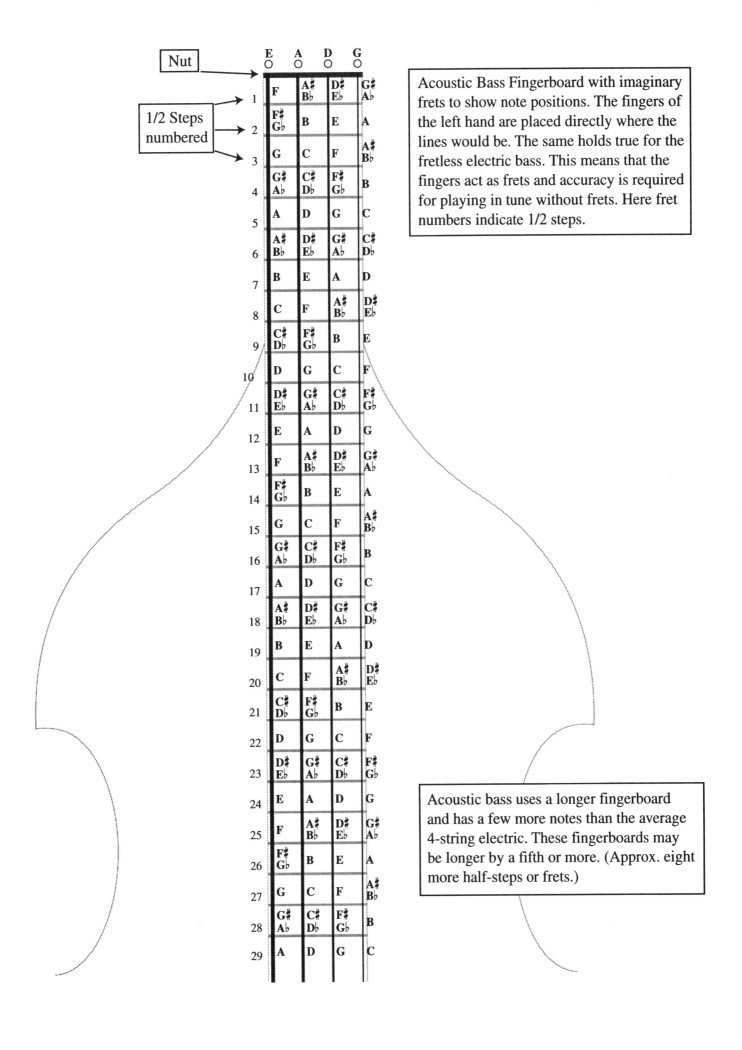

Acoustic Bass Fingerboard with imaginary frets to show note positions. The fingers of the left hand are placed directly where the lines would be. The same holds true for the fretless electric bass. This means that the fingers act as frets and accuracy is required for playing in tune without frets. Here fret numbers indicate 1/2 steps.

Acoustic bass uses a longer fingerboard and has a few more notes than the average 4-string electric. These fingerboards may be longer by a fifth or more. (Approx. eight more half-steps or frets.)

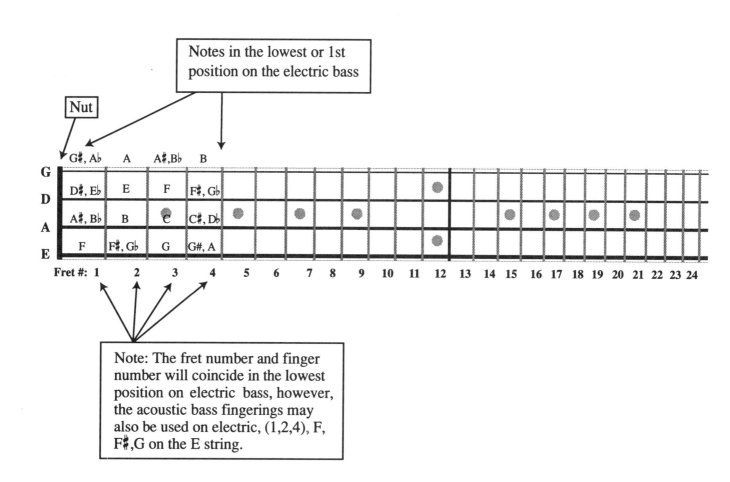

Notes in the lowest or 1st position on the electric bass

Nut

Note: The fret number and finger number will coincide in the lowest position on electric bass, however, the acoustic bass fingerings may also be used on electric, (1,2,4), F, F#,G on the E string.

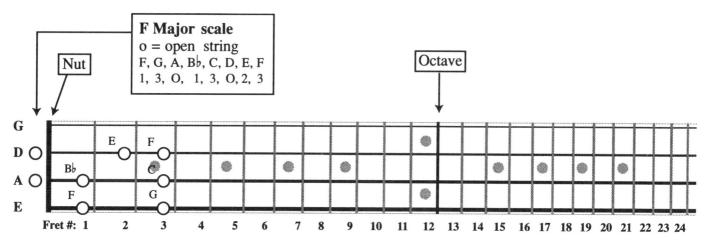

F Major scale
o = open string
F, G, A, B♭, C, D, E, F
1, 3, O, 1, 3, O, 2, 3

Nut

Octave

The lowest position on acoustic bass allows for 3 semitones, (1/2 steps), with the fingers 1, 2 and 4. To reach the 4th 1/2 step a shift is required. This is because the notes on the acoustic are further apart with the string length being around 6 inches longer.

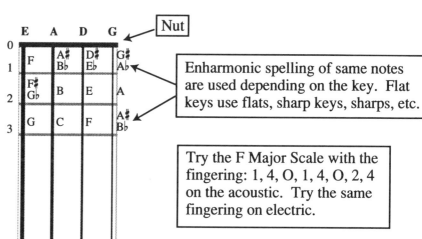

Enharmonic spelling of same notes are used depending on the key. Flat keys use flats, sharp keys, sharps, etc.

Try the F Major Scale with the fingering: 1, 4, O, 1, 4, O, 2, 4 on the acoustic. Try the same fingering on electric.

40

The Value of Reading Music

To a bassist, reading music is an extremely valuable skill to develop and perfect for many reasons. So much material exists to study and learn that becomes accessible to someone with reading skills. A tremendous amount of employment awaits the bassist who reads. Although it may be true that many musicians who do not read have work they are limited to non-reading work which is also limited. Why limit yourself? If you want to become a master just follow the steps and learn to read. Begin simple with open strings (E, A, D, G on 4 string bass).

Work with different combinations of these four notes along with rhythm exercises. Once this becomes fairly natural you're on your way. Next practice the first four notes on each individual string, each note then combined with the open string. Then combine two strings, three strings and finally four, (five and/or six later). Next are scales and triads, (some real music!), across the strings. Then comes shifting up and down the neck. Begin with scales up to the fifth, (sol), on one string, (each string), and back down.

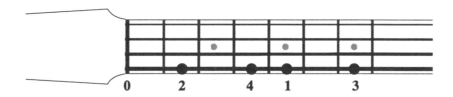

Do the same thing with all scales and arpeggios. Read them while playing them.

Next practice reading in positions and notice what positions fit certain passages based on the highest and lowest note(s). Check the interval chart and memorize all the positions in which you can play each interval. Then when reading and recognizing intervals it will be easier to play.

Learning to Read Music

Reading music is an acquired skill. Like other skills it becomes developed through practice and use. When reading music several senses are at work. Sight, Sound, Feel and Intellect.

To practice and learn reading music can be split into two elements, pitch and rhythm. Other subtleties such as dynamics, articulations and stylistic phrasing etc. will come later with more experience. In the beginning focus on pitch and rhythm. Each of these two items have their own set of challenges. With pitch it requires some knowledge of the finger board/positions along with listening skills and with rhythm it requires a consistent sense of time and the ability to subdivide it. These abilities ironically can come from practicing reading.

An effective way for beginners to practice is to separate these two elements and work on each, alone.

Lets begin with pitch. Take a simple exercise with a short range, (something that stays in the staff). Put a metronome, drum machine or other time reference on a medium pulse, approx. 72 beats/min. For now ignore the rhythm of the exercise and play each note eight times. After the first attack of each new note you have seven more beats of it to determine what the next note is and be ready to play it. You should try to determine the next note immediately since you are obviously already playing the note you're on. Play the next note for the next eight beats and be ready for the following note, etc. This exercise will teach you to look ahead in the music and reinforce pitch recognition and even time through repetition. After making it through the piece playing the notes 8 times each go through it again playing them 4 times each, shortening the time to look ahead. Then do it playing the notes 2 times and finally play it slowly with each note as a whole note, once each. Again play it with each note as a half note. Now that you've played the notes it is time to count the rhythm. See "Looking Ahead", repeated note exercises. (Book II)

With your metronome on, clap your hands in the smallest denomination of the rhythm in the piece, (1/4's, 1/8ths, 1/16ths, etc.) While clapping all of the subdivisions lightly, clap louder wherever there is a note. Do this slowly at first, then gradually build up the tempo. Some parts of the piece may be simple, while others are more complex. You may not have to use this technique on the simpler parts, however you should do whatever it takes to get the piece together. This technique is also helpful for advanced players where complicated phrases occur.

Recognition of scale sequences and rhythmic patterns as well as intervals can be a great aid to you. Try to internalize as many musical phrases as possible. When phrases reoccur it will be like a familiar sentence in a book and you will read it more readily.

Basics

The two dots indicate the note, F on the fourth line

Whole note rest means don't play for four beats.

This is a Bass Clef or "F" Clef

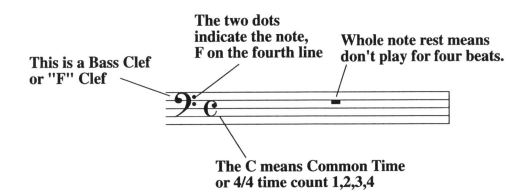

The C means Common Time or 4/4 time count 1,2,3,4

Open Strings

Whole Notes count four beats each

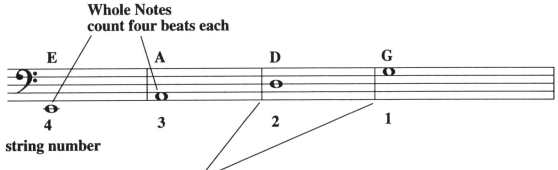

string number

Vertical lines are called Bar lines and are used to divide the staff into Measures. The Time Signature tells us how many beats are in each measure. (C or 4/4, four beats, 3/4, three beats etc.) The bottom number of the Time Signature tells us what pulse to count. (4/4 count four quarter notes, 3/8 count three eighth notes, etc.)

Bass music is written an octave higher than it actually sounds in the staff. The reason for this is to make the music easier to read. If bass music was written where it actually sounds the player would constantly be dealing with many ledger lines below the clef. The one octave transposition puts most of the bass parts right in the staff where they are practical to read

Written

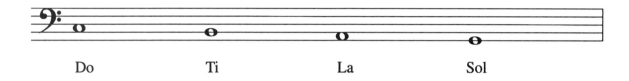

Do   Ti   La   Sol

Actual sound

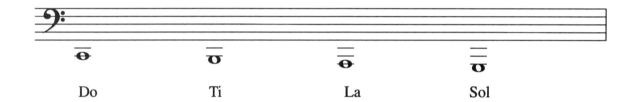

Do   Ti   La   Sol

On the keyboard below the black keys are the sharps and flats while the white keys are all naturals.

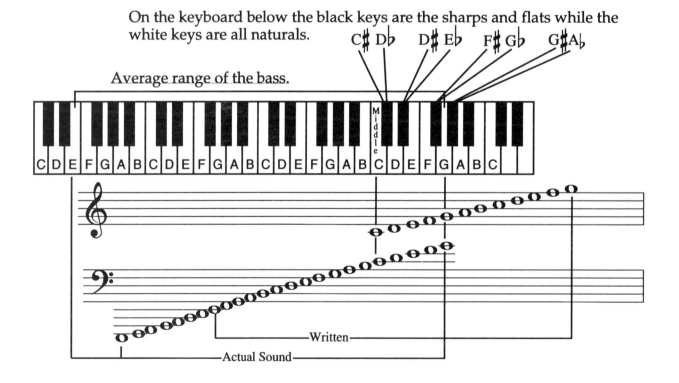

Note Values

o
1 2 3 4 .... Whole Note

1 2 3 4 .... Half Notes

1   2   3   4 .... Quarter Notes

1 & 2 & 3 & 4 & .... Eighth Notes

1 e & a 2 e & a 3 e & a 4 e & a .... Sixteenth Notes

3   3   3   3 .... Eighth Note Triplets

3   3 .... Quarter Note Triplets

3 .... Half Note Triplets

Rest Values

.... Whole Rest

.... Half Rests

.... Quarter Rests

.... Eighth Rests

.... Sixteenth Rests

3 .... Eighth Triplet Rest

3 .... Quarter Triplet Rest

3 .... Half Triplet Rest

45

Counting Notes in 4/4

Whole Note

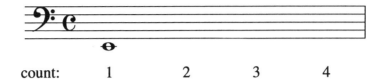

count: 1   2   3   4

Half Notes

count: 1   2   3   4

Quarter Notes

count: 1   2   3   4

Eighth Notes

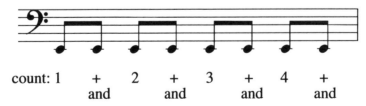

count: 1   +   2   +   3   +   4   +
        and   and   and   and

Counting Rests in 4/4

Whole Rest

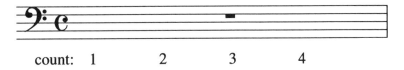

count: 1   2   3   4

Half Rests

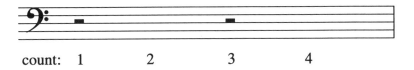

count: 1   2   3   4

Quarter Rests

count: 1   2   3   4

Eighth Rests

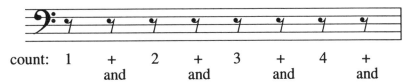

count: 1   +   2   +   3   +   4   +
                and   and   and   and

Sixteenth Notes

4 sixteenth notes equal 1 quarter note or 1 beat

count: 1   e   +   a   2   e   +   a   3   e   +   a   4   e   +   a

Eighth Note Triplets

Triplets are played 3 in the space of 2. Here 3 eighth notes in the space of 2.

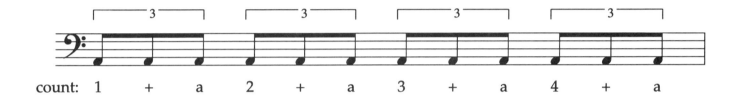

count: 1   +   a   2   +   a   3   +   a   4   +   a

Quarter Note Triplets

Like eighth note triplets quarter note triplets are played 3 quarters in the space of 2.

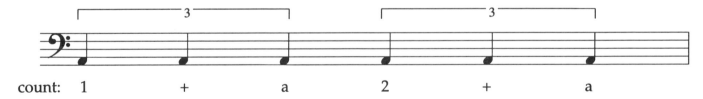

count: 1   +   a   2   +   a

Note that the easiest way to count quarter note triplets is to feel the 4/4 time in half or 2/2 with a down-beat on 1 and 3 of the 4/4 time.

Half Note Triplets

Half note triplets are difficult to count and feel particularly at slower tempos.
Thinking of four sets of eighth note triplets for each measure. Play on every 5th eighth.

count:
1/8th triplets and play on every 5th eighth note as in the accents below.

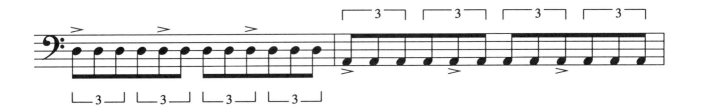

Sixteenth Rests

count: **1**   e   &   a   **2**   e   &   a   **3**   e   &   a   **4**   e   &   a

count: **1**   e   &   a   **2**   e   &   a   **3**   e   &   a   **4**   e   &   a

First clap the above rhythm and then try playing it on the bass. Combinations of notes, rests and ties can make for complex, rhythmic reading. Subdividing to the smallest note value and clapping the examples before playing them should help work the phrase(s) out. Sixteenth notes are similar to eighths in that they both divide the beat evenly in half, (multiples of 2). See the comparison below.

OPEN STRING RHYTHM STUDIES

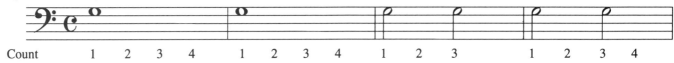

Note Values Combined

Using a metronome set at 72 beats/min. count the beats while playing the note "G"
Beat numbers, (1, 2, 3, 4) should be in sync. with metronome, +'s, (and's) fall directly in between.

open G, 1st string

open G, 1st string

Note & Rest Values Combined

Using a metronome set at 72 beats/min. count the beats of the notes and rests.
+ = and or an up-beat occurring evenly between down-beats, (metronome).

(The dotted 1/2 note below gets 3 beats.)

open D, 2nd string

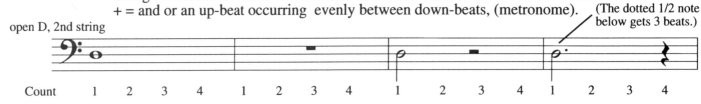

Open String Exercises

Keep the other strings quiet, damping with the left hand and unused fingers of the right hand.
Acoustic bass players should play these examples with a full bow on half and whole notes and
a half bow on quarters, stopping the bow without leaving the string, directly on the beat of each rest.

Open A, 3rd string

open E, 4th string

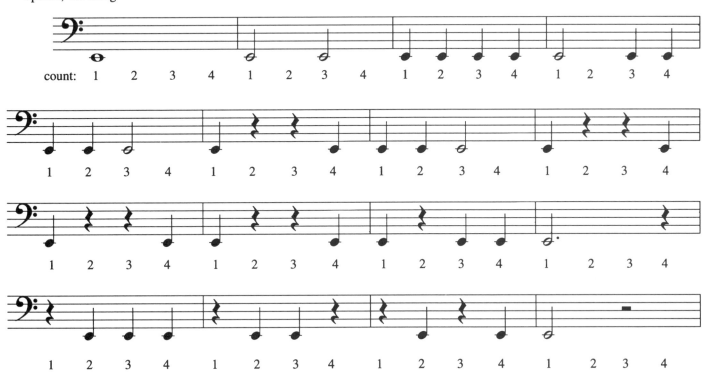

Repeat Brackets

These brackets indicate that everything between them gets repeated once for a total of two complete passes unless instructed otherwise

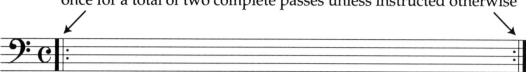

4X's   This measure gets played four times, (4X's)

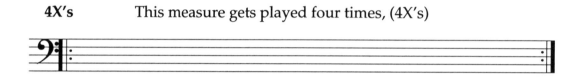

Here it is required to repeat back to the sign, (𝄋) then play to the *fine,* (end).

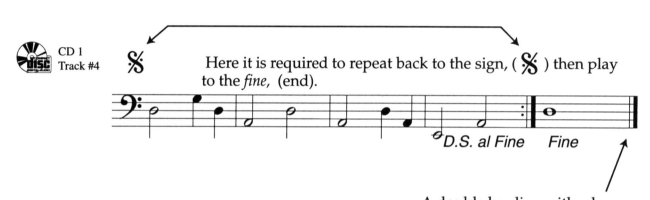

D.S. al Fine   Fine

A double bar line with a heavy final line marks the end as does *Fine.*

A coda sign is much like a *fine* however a coda can be an entire, final, section of music and include a *Fine* at the very end.

D.S. al Coda   Fine

Open Strings

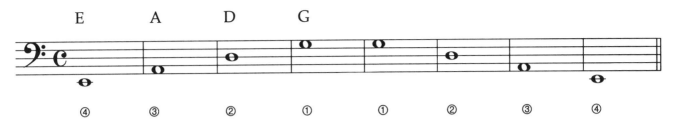

Practice the following open string exercises with a metronome giving you four beats per measure. Be sure to damp the other strings and achieve a clean sound with an even attack.

CD 1
Track #5

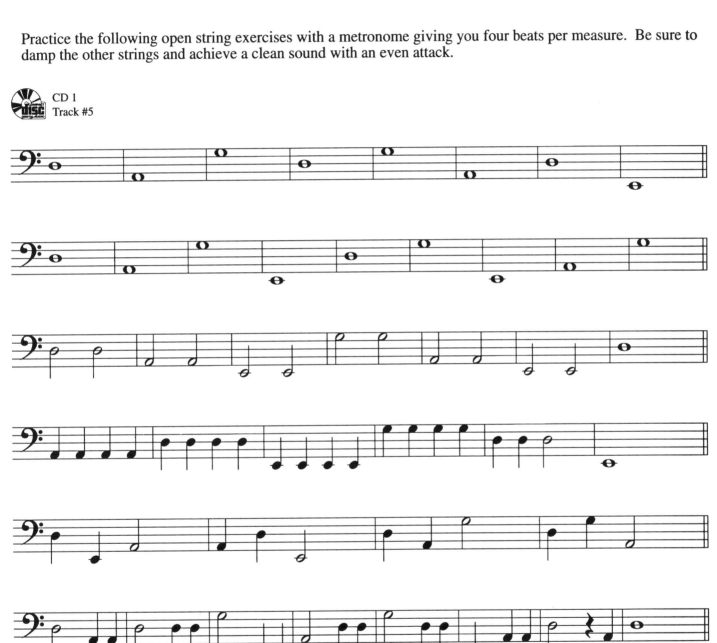

Open Strings Rhythm Studies

Open Strings Rhythm Studies Continued
(Adjacent)

Adjacent and Non-adjacent Open Strings
Rhythm Studies

Open Strings Rhythm Studies Continued
(Adjacent)

Clap rhythms before playing

rt=root of chord
5th=fifth of chord

count: 1 & 2 & 3 & 4 &

-Rhythm & Blues-

A7　　　　　D7　　　　　A7　　　　　E7

-Reggae-

Amin　　　　　　　　Dmin

Dmin　　　　　　　　Gmin

rt　　　5th　　　rt　　　5th　　　rt　　　5th　　　rt　　　5th

Time Signatures

The top number tells us how many beats per measure and the bottom number tells us what kind of note value to count for each beat. Note how each measure below contains a full count of notes equal to its time signature. **Downbeats** are extremely important as they mark the beginning of each measure and help to keep us from losing the beat and/or getting lost in the music.

Dotted Note Values
in 4/4 Time

A dot following a note increases its length by half its value. The dotted quarter
is 1 1/2 beats and the dotted half note is 3 beats. A dotted eighth note is 3/4 of a beat.

1.

count: 1   &   2   &   3   &   4   &   1   &   2   &   3   &   4   &

note, when played at a fast tempo, example 2, (the dotted half followed by a quarter),
sounds similar to the dotted quarter followed by the eighth in example 1.

2.

count: 1   2   3   4   1   2   3   4

Example 3, (dotted eighth, sixteenth note rhythm), is also a similar relationship
with smaller note values. These are all ways of subdividing time into different
size parts or fractions. Subdividing time into rhythm is an essential skill for any
instrumentalist.

3.

count: 1 e & a   2 e & a 3 e & a 4 e & a   1 e & a 2 e & a 3 e & a 4 e & a

Example 4 is like examlpe 1 however there is an eighth rest on beat 2 which means
the first 1/2 of beat 2 is silent. Placing your picking finger on the string at beat 2 will
silence the string and prepare you for the & of 2.

4.

count: 1   &   2   &   3   &   4   &   1   &   2   &   3   &   4   &

Dotted Rests

Occasionally dotted values are added to rests, but additional rests are easier to read.

Dotted Note Values
in other Time Signatures

Open Strings Rhythm Studies Continued
(Adjacent)

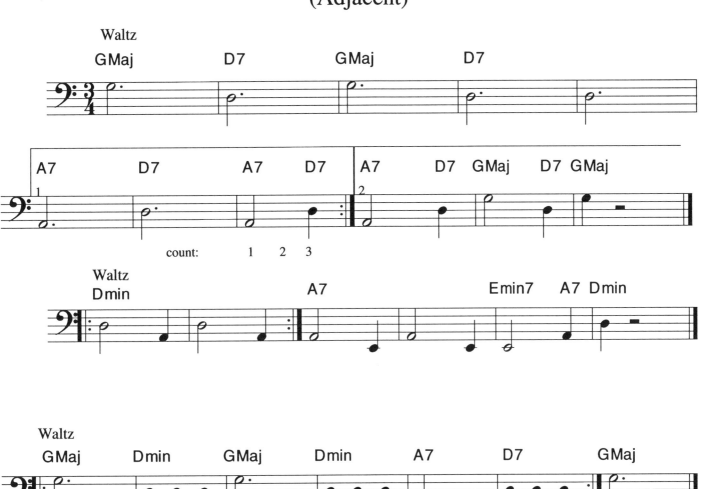

-Rock-

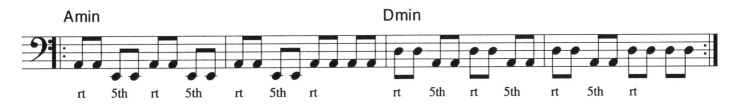

The Tie

After the attack of the first note it should sustain for the duration of the full tied value.
Example 1. is 8 beats. Example 2. is 5 beats. Example 3. is 2 beats. Ex.4 is 1 1/2 beats.

1.

2.

2 beat tie

3.

4.

Note how this is the same rhythm as example 4.

G & D

Note how #4 and #3 are similar with #4 being twice as many beats, 8ths rather than quarters.
If you were to play #3 twice as fast it would sound like #4 rhythmically.

Ties indicate a sustained note
for the tied, combined values.

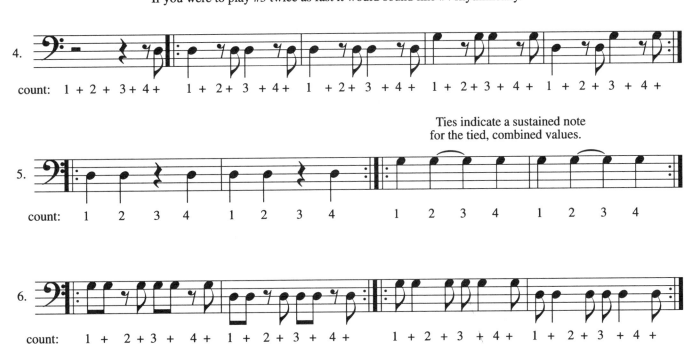

G & D cont'd

Similar Rhythms

Note how measures 2 & 3 are the same as measures 1 & 4. They are two ways of notating the same rhythm

Triplets are three to a beat and counted 1+ a 2 + a 3 + a 4 + a

Open Strings Rhythm Studies Continued

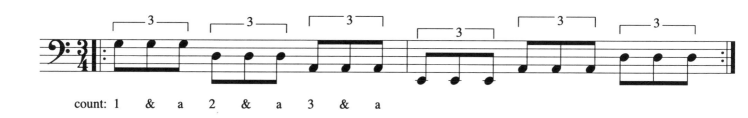

count: 1   &   a   2   &   a   3   &   a

count: 1   2   3   4   5   6   7   8   9

The Beat or Groove

In much the same way we use clocks to delineate time in milliseconds, seconds, minutes, hours, days, weeks, months, etc., music uses sound and silence to delineate time. The units used in music are subdivisions of beats, (64ths, 32nds, 16ths, 8ths, 4ths, or quarters, 1/2's and wholes), which are then grouped in measures or bars. The measures put together create phrases which are then combined yielding longer phrases and eventually sections of whole song forms. A beat is one pulse at a designated tempo or speed. When sound and silence are aligned to a beat in time they create rhythm.

The second hand on a clock moves at 60 beats per minute. Musicians use a metronome or other adjustable time reference to practice a steady pulse. Metronomes can click at various tempos marked as beats per minute, (BPM). At the beginning of a piece of music is a tempo marking. These markings can be MM 92 meaning metronome marking 92 beats per minute or♩=92 (a half note is occurring 92 times per minute.) Often times in traditional music Latin terms are used such as adagio, (slow), allegro, (medium to fast), presto, (fast), and many others. These Latin terms give a tempo range rather than a specific metronome marking.

Practice with a metronome or other time device is good for developing a strong sense of time, however master musicians have internalized the time and can move all around it while the listener still feels it. After years of practice and experience we become more confident and free within the framework of the time.

Each beat has different parts, the front, the back, the sides, the center and all places in between. The front of the beat is the first to be heard and the back is the last. Because the bass is often slower speaking than other instruments it is good to play toward the front of the beat. This is known as "on top of the beat." There are different degrees of "on top" or "behind". "Behind the beat" is generally not a good place for the bass, however, in a playing situation it is relative to the drums. If you try to play on different parts of the beat you will feel the differences. It is important that you strive for consistency.

Vamps

Vamps are repeated rhythmic parts or sections in a piece of music. It means the bass is sort of in a holding pattern. Most of the open rhythm exercises could be used as vamps. Also any idea that works well repeated could be a vamp. They are often used on introductions and endings of tunes. Occasionally only chord symbols are given and the instructions, "Vamp," (meaning to maintain the groove of the piece over the given chord progression.

When playing/reading vamps there is an opportunity to learn phrase recognition and work on your groove.

Many bass parts/grooves are repetitive and for that reason I have included many short repeated examples in this book. In addition my idea is to help you build a strong time feel in a variety of rhythmic styles. The simpler/shorter the idea, the easier it is to learn and play.

Duration

Players use different durations to articulate the best possible feel/groove for the piece. Often a half may be short or a quarter note long, making them similar. See the examples below.

Open Strings Rhythm Studies Continued

skipping strings

-Shuffle-

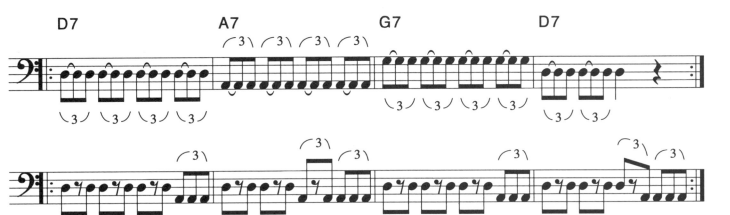

-Walking bass rhythm-

Open Strings Rhythm Studies Continued

-Reggae-

-On the beat and off the beat-

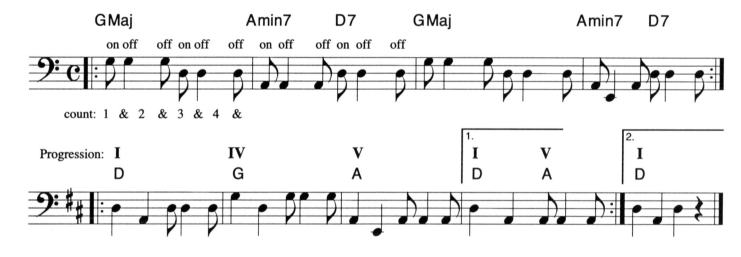

Triplets

Bolero

Open Strings Rhythm Studies Continued

-Rock & Roll-

even 8th note time

note: 50's rock is sometimes like mambo

-Motown-

note: 12/8 feels like triplets in 4/4

Open Strings Rhythm Studies Continued

-Stinging Rock, even time-

The following example uses a 1st and 2nd ending. Play to the 1st ending,
repeat back to the repeat sign, then skip the 1st ending and play the 2nd.

-Baroque (even)-

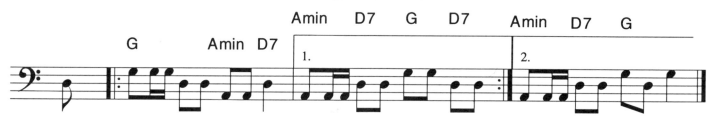

-Shuffle: ♫ = ♩♪ ³ -

-Funk with ties-

Reminder: clap rhythm before playing.

Open Strings Minor Blues, Funk Style

Also try playing this exercise with the notes A and D on the 5th fret

90 BPM
Quarter note

After playing the D blues below with open strings, play it with all the notes
at the 5th fret, then try combinations of open strings and 5th fret notes.

Open String Rhythms Continued

sixteenths   note: maintain 16th count/feel through rests etc.

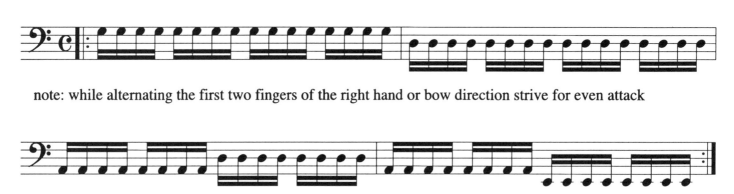

note: while alternating the first two fingers of the right hand or bow direction strive for even attack

count: 1 e & a 2 e & a 3 e & a 4 e & a   1 e & a 2 e & a 3 e & a 4 e & a

syncopation, notes and rests combined on up beats and down beats

count: 1   e   & a   2   e   & a   3   e   & a   4   e   & a

-Funk-

Right Hand Exercise

Alternate the 1st & 2nd fingers of the right hand while keeping the un-played strings, quiet with the left hand. Accentuate the downbeats. Strive for even attacks while working up the tempo. This should also prove to be a good exercise for bowing the upright bass. For now play alternating down bow up bow.

Right Hand Radiation Exercises Continued

TIME AND RHYTHM

Time
Music in time and your internal clock

Of all the elements of music, time and rhythm are to a bassist what water and sunshine are to living things. Without a beat music loses its physical motion. Combinations of attacks and durations of both sound and silence through time create rhythm. Generally in most styles of music a consistent pulse is desirable. One can dance, tap their feet or clap their hands to a good, steady beat. This may have something to do with our internal clock, (pulse), heart beat, etc. We all have a somewhat consistent rhythm pumping our blood through our veins. This may be why music in time is the most popular. As the bass is the fundamental bottom voice of music it is most supportive in an even steady beat. Each of the many styles of music presents a different rhythmic challenge to a bassist and only through experience can he or she articulate all these styles.

One essential experience to all musicians is listening. Not only do bass players need to listen to other instruments, but how they fit into the music with those instruments. Listening carefully to recordings is one of the best and enjoyable learning tools a player can have. With the wealth of material available one can find almost any style to study/enjoy. While listening to recordings pay attention to the bass and hear its relationship to the drums and other instruments. In Pop, Blues, Jazz, Funk, Reggae, Rock, R&B, Country, Baroque, etc. (combos), the bass and drums are almost always forming a synchronized rhythm called a groove. Music "grooves" when it moves through time in a consistent fashion. In Symphonic, Chamber, Traditional, Classical and other so called legitimate styles the beat is not always as prevalent as in popular music. Conductors of orchestras can stretch and squeeze beats/phrases to create personal effects. Types of Jazz music can also have flexible time.

Music is in time most of the time and therefore bassists must be reliable time players providing the pulse and the bass/foundation of the harmony.

How to Practice Time

There are many ways to practice time.

1. Using a metronome is helpful for hearing a reference of steady time. Try practicing simple ideas with the metronome on a medium pulse, (72 or so) and let that pulse represent quarter notes. Play one measure of music and rest for the next while listening to the beat of a metronome. Each time you come back in to play, every other measure lock in your time with the metronome. Begin in 4/4 time and play the same note as four quarter notes, synchronizing your attack, (right hand), with the beat. After that feels comfortable try two notes, twice each, (E, E, G, G). When playing notes on the neck, the fingers of the left hand must be on the desired notes a bit early to get a good solid tone when the attack is made. These exercises are to be repeated until it feels like you are grooving.

PLAY	REST	PLAY	REST
LISTEN	LISTEN	LISTEN	LISTEN
1, 2, 3, 4	1, 2, 3, 4	1, 2, 3, 4	1, 2, 3, 4

After practicing with the metronome on all 4 beats practice putting the metronome on beats 1 and 3 only then 2 and 4 only. Later try only beat 1. Only beat 2, only beat 3 and only beat 4. You'll need to slow down the tempo of the metronome for practicing only 1 beat. Practicing up-beats is another good exercise. The and of 1, and of 2, 3 or and of 4.

1 & 2 & 3 & 4 &   1 & 2 & 3 & 4 &   1 & 2 & 3 & 4 &   1 & 2 & 3 & 4 &

Rhythmic figures are good to practice. See the rhythmic notation pages. Four bar phrases with the metronome can help you feel time like good drummers. You can combine rhythmic figures with walking bass or vamps by playing accents to outline the figures.

2. Practice with recordings. This will give you the feeling of real musicians time which is much more practical than a metronome. Hopefully you'll be playing with musicians more than metronomes. There are great recordings in just about every style of music for you to play along with and hook up.

3. Play with other musicians. Practice, rehearse and perform with others as much as possible. This is the best experience you can get.

4. Internal singing or singing out loud of rhythms and phrases can help you build a strong sense of time.

5. Invent your own rhythm and time exercises.

Time and Rhythmic Accuracy

Time and rhythmic accuracy can be improved/perfected through various exercises and conceptual approaches. Exercise 1. Using a metronome or other time reference beating four beats to the bar, not too fast at first, play one note beginning on the downbeat. Rest for the remainder of that bar and the following bar listening to the time. After you've mastered an accurate attack on that beat practice the 2nd beat, then the third and finally the fourth.

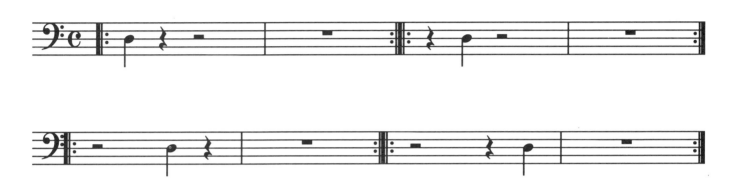

Now do the same exercise with the eighth note positions in the bar. Use the metronome on both quarter note and eighth note pulse.

Time and Rhythmic Accuracy Continued

Now play each of the twelve positions of eighth note triplets.

Syncopations

In the following examples tap your foot 4 beats to the bar. When your foot is down, play the on/down beats, and when is up, play the off/up beats.

Rhythmic Notation of Common Bass Grooves

THEORY

Sharps (♯) raise a note by one half step or one fret.

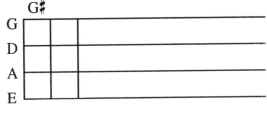

Fret: 0   1   2

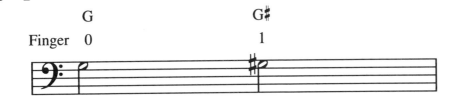

Flats (♭) lower a note by one half step or one fret.

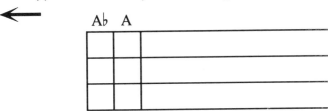

Fret: 0   1   2

Key Signatures

Key signatures are placed at the beginning of a piece of music. They tell us which notes are going to be sharp or flat. Usually pieces are in a sharp or flat key to begin with. The examples below show the key of D, (2(♯)'s) and the key of B♭, (2♭'s).

Accidentals are (♯)'s, ♭'s or ♮'s which are placed before notes to change them up or down 1/2 step to notes not in the key signature. They are also used to return notes to the key signature. See the example below. The key is D and we are using a ♮ sign to change F natural then a (♯) to change back to F sharp. Accidentals apply to all notes of that pitch for the remainder of the measure unless otherwise indicated with another accidental as in the example.

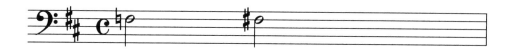

Sometimes music is written without a key signature for various reasons, (changes key often, isn't in a particular key etc.)

Also there exists a double sharp, (✕), to raise a note one whole step, (two half-steps), and a double flat, (♭♭), to lower pitch by a whole step. When a key signature is used all the notes that are sharp or flat in the signature are to be played that way unless accidentals are used to tell you otherwise. On the following page is a chart of the fifteen key signatures. Although there are really only twelve sounding keys in western music, three of the keys have two different spellings, (enharmonic spellings), bringing the total written keys to fifteen.

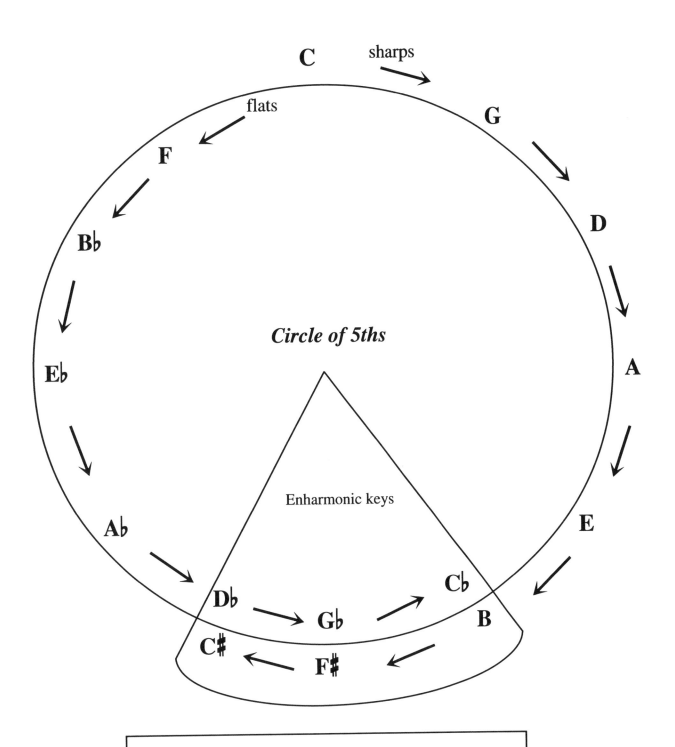

Circle of 5ths

Enharmonic keys

Add sharps in the following order: F C G D A E B

Add flats in the following order: B E A D G C F

Key Signature Chart

Key	Number of sharps/flats	Order of sharps/flats	Key Signature
C♯ Major/A♯ minor	7 sharps	FCGDAEB	
F♯ Major/ D♯ minor	6 sharps	FCGDAE	
B Major/ G♯ minor	5 sharps	FCGDA	
E Major/ C♯ minor	4 sharps	FCGD	
A Major/ F♯ minor	3 sharps	FCG	
D Major/ B minor	2 sharps	FC	
G Major/ E minor	1 sharp	F	
C Major/ A minor	0 sharps/flats	None	
F Major/ D minor	1 flat	B	
B♭ Major/ G minor	2 flats	BE	
E♭ Major/ C minor	3 flats	BEA	
A♭ Major/ F minor	4 flats	BEAD	
D♭ Major/ B♭ minor	5 flats	BEADG	
G♭ Major/ E♭ minor	6 flats	BEADGC	
C♭ Major/ A♭ minor	7 flats	BEADGCF	

Intervals of the Chromatic Scale Expanding by 1/2 Steps

As we increase the distance between notes (interval), by 1/2 steps the intervals become greater while decreasing the distance, reduces the interval. Observe the position of these intervals shown. Memorize them and try other fingerings using the "Note Finder Diagrams" if necessary. Sing the intervals and internalize their sounds.

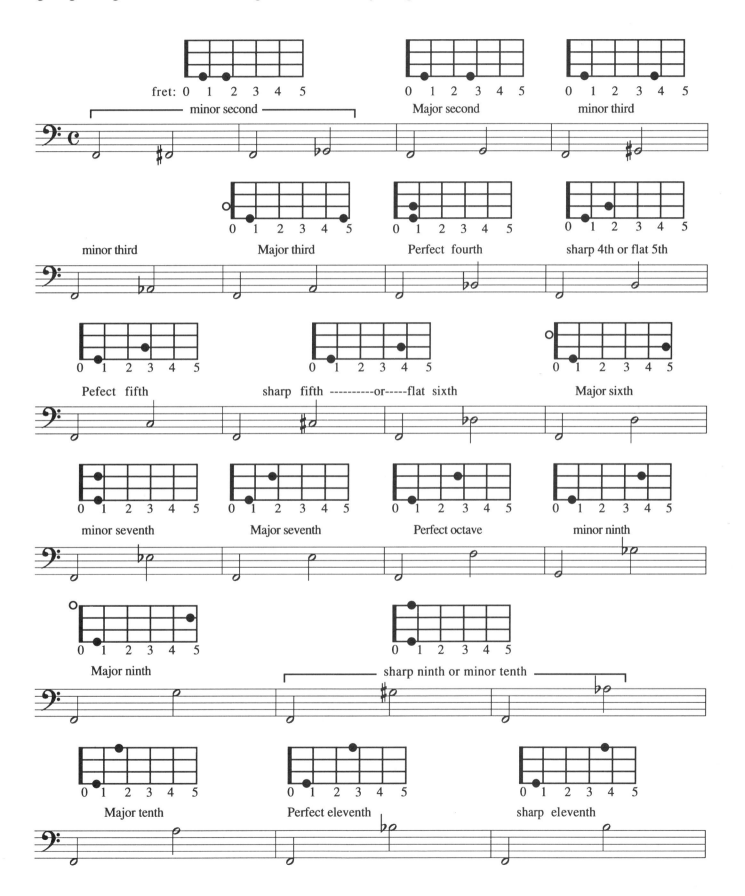

Major Scale Construction

The major scale is made up of a series of whole steps (2 frets) and half steps (1 fret) as follows: whole, whole, half, whole, whole, whole, half. (1=whole step, 1/2=half step)

G Major

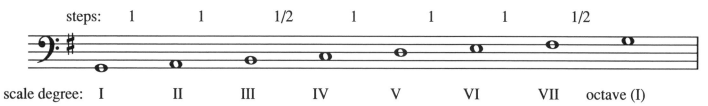

steps:	1	1	1/2	1	1	1	1/2

scale degree:	I	II	III	IV	V	VI	VII	octave (I)

G Major fingered with open strings in first position (bass guitar), second position (upright bass)

E. finger:	3	0	2	3	0	2	4	0
A. finger:	2	0	1	2	0	1	4	0

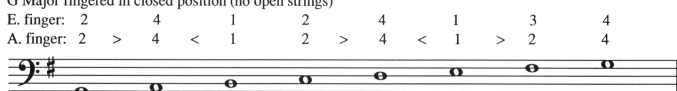

G Major fingered in closed position (no open strings)

E. finger:	2		4		1	2		4		1		3	4
A. finger:	2	>	4	<	1	2	>	4	<	1	>	2	4

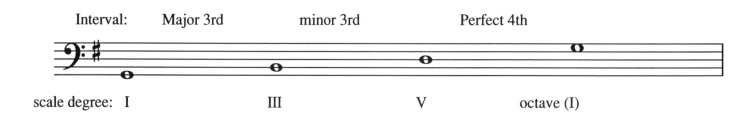

Construction of the Major Triad is a Major third followed by a minor third and a perfect fourth or simply the root, 3rd, 5th and octave of the Major scale.

Interval:	Major 3rd	minor 3rd	Perfect 4th

scale degree:	I	III	V	octave (I)

Minor Scale Construction

The minor scale is made up of a series of whole steps (2 frets) and half steps (1 fret) as follows: whole, half, whole, whole, half, whole, whole (1=whole step, 1/2=half step). If you start the major scale on the sixth step and play a full octave you are playing the natural, relative minor scale. Other minor scale forms can be found in "110 Scales in First Position" and the "Theory" section of Mastering the Bass II.

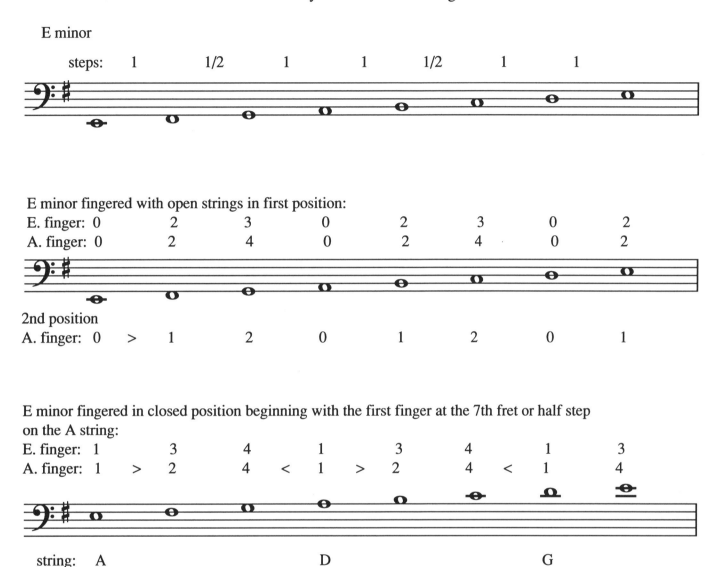

E minor

steps: 1   1/2   1   1   1/2   1   1

E minor fingered with open strings in first position:

| E. finger: | 0 | 2 | 3 | 0 | 2 | 3 | 0 | 2 |
| A. finger: | 0 | 2 | 4 | 0 | 2 | 4 | 0 | 2 |

2nd position

A. finger: 0 > 1   2   0   1   2   0   1

E minor fingered in closed position beginning with the first finger at the 7th fret or half step on the A string:

| E. finger: | 1 | | 3 | | 4 | | 1 | | 3 | | 4 | | 1 | | 3 |
| A. finger: | 1 | > | 2 | | 4 | < | 1 | > | 2 | | 4 | < | 1 | | 4 |

string: A   D   G

Construction of the minor triad is a minor third followed by a Major third and a perfect fourth or simply the root, 3rd, 5th and octave of the minor scale.

Interval: minor 3rd   Major 3rd   Perfect 4th

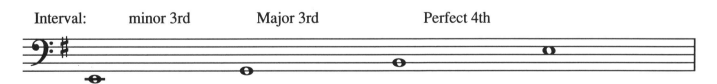

Intervals of a Major Scale

Counting up from C, (1) we have four major, (M), intervals and three perfect, (P), intervals. They are measured by diatonic, (relative to scale), whole steps, (W) and half steps, (H). The step-wise and intervallic construction of the major scale is the same regardless of the key. Whole steps are major intervals and half steps are minor intervals. A major scale has five whole steps between, (1-2, 2-3, 4-5, 5-6 and 6-7), and two half steps between, (3-4 and 7-8).

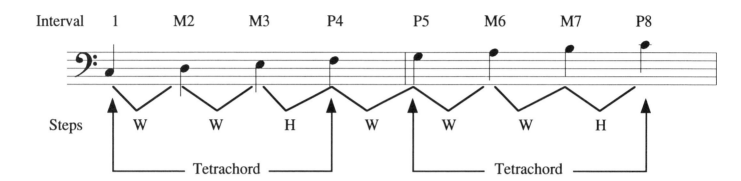

Scales can be divided into two Tetrachords. The word Tetra means four. From C to F is one tetrachord and from G to C, (an octave above), is the second tetrachord. In a major scale both tetrachords are constructed whole step, whole step, half step with a whole step joining the two tetrachords.

Scale Degrees

When counting up from the root, (1), note that the scale degree is the same number as the interval from (1). The intervals between the scale degrees are (M), Major 2nds or (m), minor 2nds, (the interval names for whole steps and half steps).

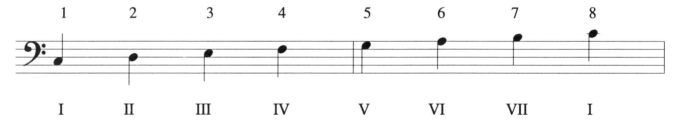

Roman numerals are used for harmony built upon the scale degrees
For purposes of harmonic analysis 8, (the octave), is called I

Interval Piece

2nds & 5ths

Grooves with 4ths & 5ths

93

1ST POSITION

First 5 Notes on the E String (4)

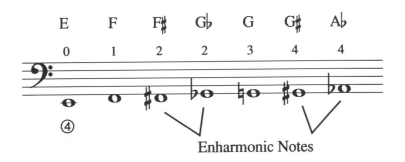

Exercises on the E String (4), (1st position, 1st 5 notes only)

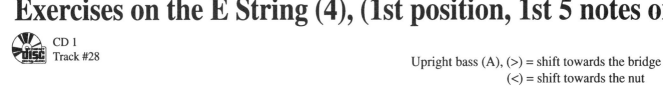

CD 1
Track #28

Upright bass (A), (>) = shift towards the bridge
(<) = shift towards the nut

Note: B♭, E♭, A♭ and D♭ are flat as indicated in the key signature. Here the key is F minor

E String Exercises Continued

Chromatic Funk

Reggae

Walking

E String Exercises Continued

Walking

Hemeola = A consistant rhythm which crosses the existing rhythm. Here it's 3/4 on 4/4

Funk

First 5 Notes on the A String (3)

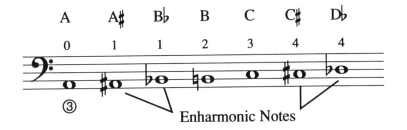

Exercises on the A String (3), (first 5 notes only)

CD 1
Track #31

CD 1
Track #32

chromatic

A minor

A Major

R & B

C7

A 7 Funk

Db 7 Funk

Bb minor

C7   A7   C7   A7

A Major, Exercise on the E & A String

CD 1
Track #34

Walking blues, bass lines in first position on the A & E strings only

C Blues

F Blues

First 5 Notes on the D String (2)

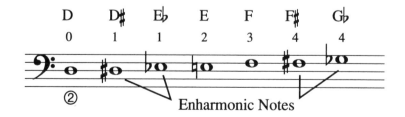

Exercises on the D String (2)
(1st 5 notes only)

(>) = shift towar ds the bridge
(<) = shift towar ds the nut

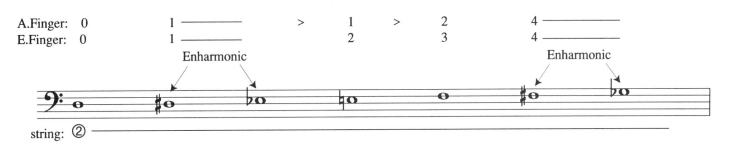

E minor with chromaticism

Eb minor

Exercises on the D String Continued

106

Walking blues bass lines in first position on the D & A strings only

F Blues

B♭ Blues

Crossing Strings

First 5 Notes on the G String (1)

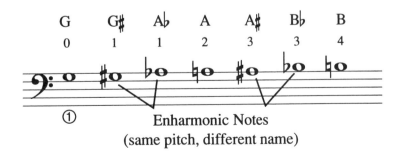

Exercises on the G String (1),
(1st 5 notes only)

Exercises on the G String Continued

Enharmonic Spelling

When a note of the same pitch has different names they are called enharmonic spellings. For example raising the note G by one half step yields G sharp and lowering the note A by one half step gives us A flat. This means that G sharp and A flat are enharmonic spellings for the same note. See examples below:

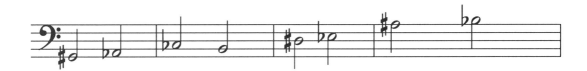

The following is a musical example using enharmonic spellings. Note how when a note descends it is flat and when it ascends it is sharp. This is often how music is written however there are exceptions and key signatures will also play a part in naming notes properly.

CD 1
Track #41

Enharm's Way

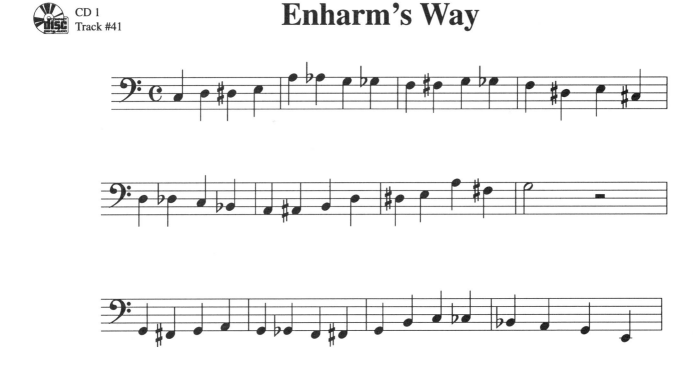

Walking blues bass lines in first position on the G & D strings only

Bb Blues

For a faster tempo try Disc 2, Tracks 8 & 9

Eb Blues

Tie Exercises

Never Say Never

Waltz
legato, smooth

B. Gertz

F# Dorian Scale

| E.Finger: | 2 | 4 | 0 | 2 | 4 | 1 | 2 | 4 |
| A.Finger: | 1 | 4 | 0 | 1 | 4 < | 1 | 2 > | 4 |

Drunken Sailor

Dorian Modal Piece

Question and Answer

Measure 1 is a question and measure 2 an answer. The phrases in this piece are of this nature.

E Dorian

Battle of Jericho

Shuffle like feel

− = Long
∧ = Short

After reading the melody try improvising over it.

1st Position 2nd Finger (A)

1st Position 2nd Finger (E)

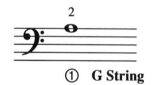

① G String

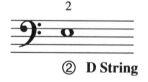

② D String

Some players find it more comfortable to use upright bass fingerings in the low positions on bass guitar where the notes are further apart. Note below the span between the 1st and 4th fingers is only 3 frets rather than 4.

Perfect 5th Interval

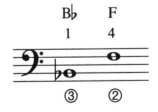

Perfect 5th Interval

119

Basic Slap Style, Right Hand

Slapping the string with the side of the thumb near the knuckle creates a percussive attack, pulling the G string with the index finger so it snaps back against the fingerboard is also very percussive. Combinations of these two techniques and hammered notes with the left hand can bring out many funky grooves and syncopations.

The thumb slapping the string over the fretboard creates a metallic sound.

Play this example with finger style first, then try playing it slap style
with the right thumb.

G Funk Blues

Progression I

Never Been Better

for Instrumental Duet

B. Gertz

Medium bossa

Live musicians on the track include Bob Kaufman, Drums, Russell Hoffman, Piano and Bruce Gertz, Bass

God Bless America
Duet

Also try playing the parts up one or two octaves.

CD 1
Track #51

My Bonnie Lies Over The Ocean
For Bass Duet

Try playing the duets up an octave. Also try singing the melody while playing the bottom part.

EAR TRAINING

Musical Ears

Sing everything you play and try to play everything you sing. Don't be shy about singing. It will make a big difference in your playing. Master musicians are singing with their instruments all the time. Your ears are at least 50% of your musical ability. If you can't sing it, you probably shouldn't play it.

To improve your ears, try to figure out and play your favorite bass parts from recordings. This will greatly improve your musical ear and bass playing. When your reading is good enough to hear what you see or visa versa, try "transcribing", (writing down), some bass parts. Since the bass usually plays roots of chords you can map out the roots of the chord progression and later figure out the chord qualities, (major, minor, dominant, etc.) Keep singing the parts.

Experiment with the CD and try to figure out the parts and write them down. Then try playing it using both your ear and the music.

Good Job!

Ear Training:
Rhythmic Dictation Exercise #1

Listen to the play-along CD and figure out the root and rhythm. Notice the phrases (2 & 4 bars each). Using a pencil, write it down below in the given staves. Try reading it and playing along with and without the bass track. Fix mistakes until it is perfect.

Ear Training:
Rhythmic Dictation Exercise #2

Like exercise #1, listen to the play-along CD and transcribe the bass part. Now you will hear more than one note (roots and fifths) and more rhythmic variation.

Ear Training: Pitch Exercise #1

Play the bass notes and sing the same note. Because the bass is so low you will probably be singing one octave higher. Simply match the pitch with your voice.

Play and let ring while singing.

Ear Training: Pitch Exercise #2

While the bass note is ringing sing another note above it, then try to play it on the bass. Then change your bass note and sing another note and find that note on the bass. After doing the single note for a while, try singing two notes and playing them, then three and four and eventually an entire phrase. This will teach you to listen to the relationship between the top voice and the bass.

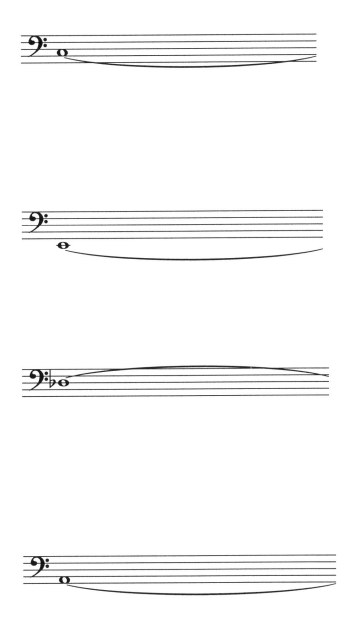

Ear Training:
Harmonic/Rhythmic Dictation

From the play-along CD, figure out the bass part with the changing harmony (chords) and the rhythm. Write down the roots, fifths and rhythms you hear. Use a pencil and fix mistakes until it is perfect. Play and read the parts. Write what you think the chords are.

1.

2.

3.

4.

PENTATONIC SCALES

E Major Pentatonic Scale

A Major Pentatonic

Use same fingering as E pentatonic starting on the A string

E Minor Pentatonic

A Minor Pentatonic

F Major Pentatonic

B♭ Major Pentatonic

Because the above scales are parallel on adjacent strings the same fingerings will work for E and A or F and B♭.

Pentatonic Piece

Pentatonic basslines

Rock

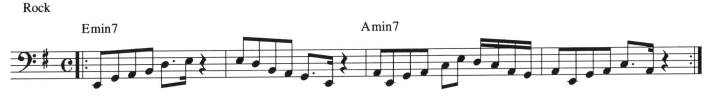

Rock/Blues shuffle

The above basslines work well on Blues progressions. Try playing the grooves on a I IV V progression.

NOTE FINDER
FINGERBOARD DIAGRAMS

Music vs the Fingering

The music is always more important than the fingering. Many players/students get too dependent upon finger patterns. For this and other reasons mentioned I have emphasized a long workout in the open positions. There will be many times when the music will sound the best played a certain way. If you rely on your limited finger patterns it may force you to miss the best sounding way to perform the passage. One should always try to get the best sound of every note. This requires knowing all the locations of the notes and the different sound qualities of the same notes in different locations on the fingerboard. On a four string, electric or acoustic bass low "F" is only available on the "E" string, one half step above the open string. The "F" one octave above that low F has three locations. Study the fingerboard charts with your hand on the bass and see where all the notes can be played. The more options you have, the better.

Note Finder Diagrams

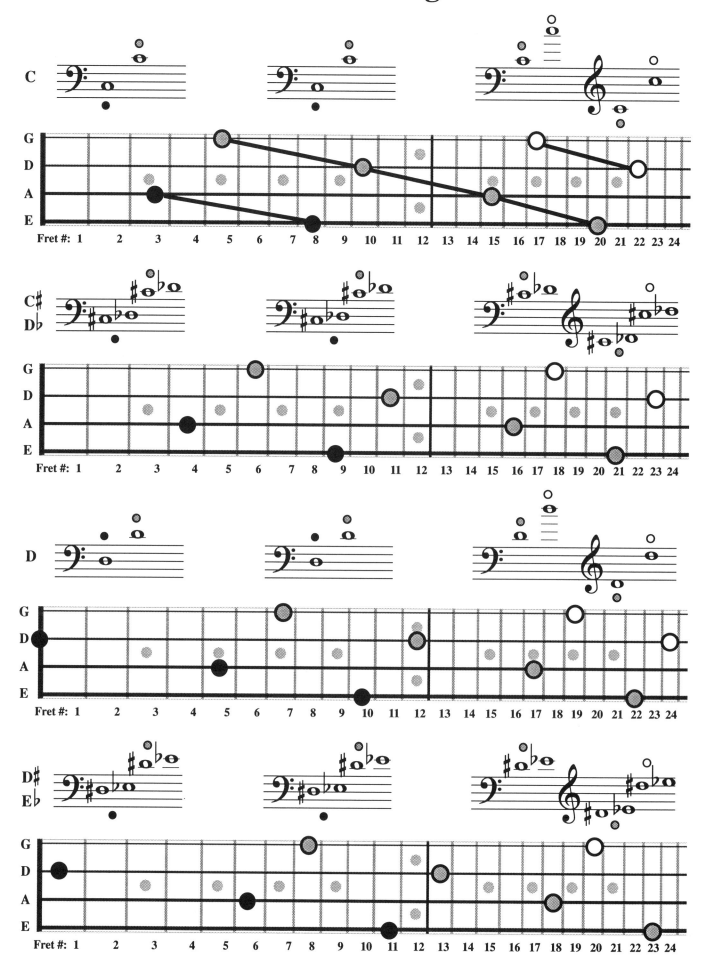

138

Note Finder Diagrams

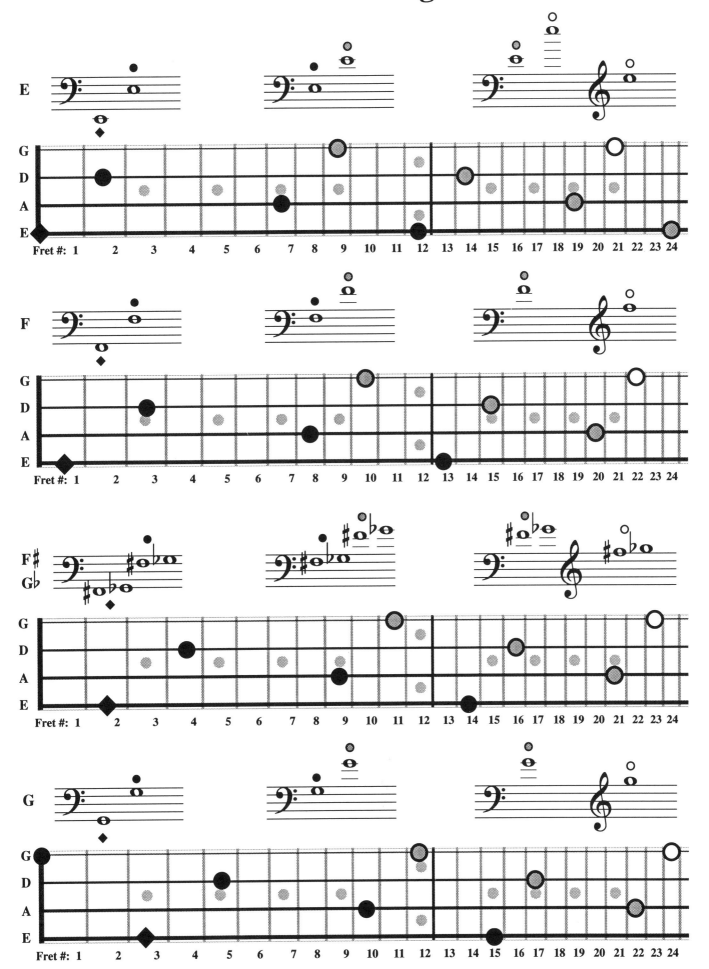

Note Finder Diagrams

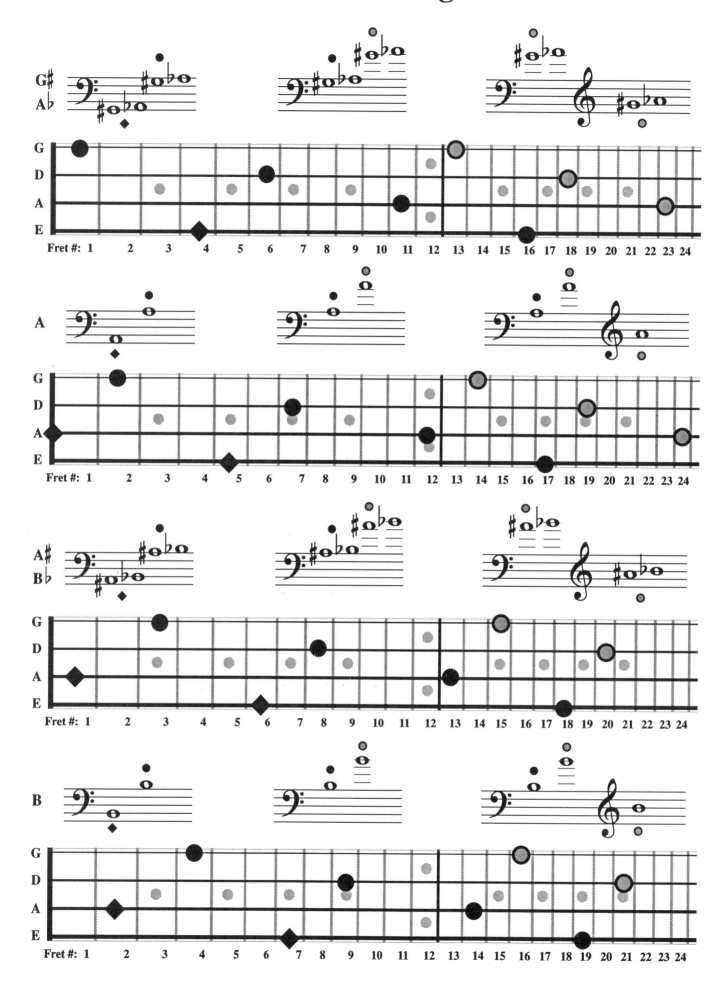

Variations on a Funky Theme

E-7 (Dorian)

Play the above variations in both the low (1st position and 4th position) with open E as the botton note. Notice how it may play out easier in 4th position because the string crossing is less complex.

Play the same variations (Funk) in A minor using the fourth position fingerings on the upper 3 strings.

141

ROOTS, 5THS, OCTAVES
BASIC CHORD CHART READING

Rhythmic Notation With
Chord Symbols and Notes (roots)

Play/read the roots of the chords in the rhythms notated.

1st x Swing x 2nd x Straight

Waltz

1st x Straight 2nd x Swing

143

Rhythmic Notation
With Chord Symbols

Play the roots of the chords in the rhythms notated.

144

Intervals in Position (Upright Bass)

Perfect 5th

Perfect 4th

Note how the 4th is played here, barring the notes under the index (1) finger. Another way is to play the A♭ with the second finger (hand rotated).

Roots & Fifths

The **Root/Fifth** bass part is one of the most commonly used bass parts in the world. It's found in virtually every style of music. Therefore it is essential to bassists. While it is one of the simplest, melodic, bass parts it can be rhytmically complex. This type of bass part will fit all chord types with only an occasional alteration of one half step up or down. If the chord is augmented the fifth should be raised 1/2 step if diminished it should be lowered 1/2 step. The following music chart shows all the chord types built on the root, **C.**

CD 2
Track #6

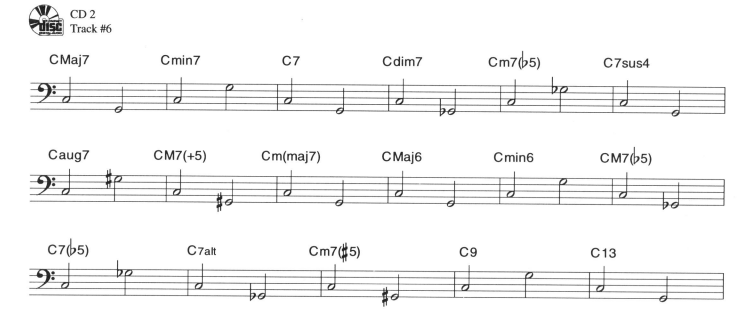

There are many different chord spellings including upper notes called tensions (usually 9, 11 and 13), which are the scale tones 2, 4 and 6 up one octave, placing them above the chord tones.

The following example shows a C Maj 7 +11 chord from the bottom up with 9,+11 and 13. Although it is important to know all the chord tones, chord scales and tensions a simple root, fifth bass part is often all that is needed. See "How to Interpret Chord Symbols". (in Mastering The Bass, Book 2)

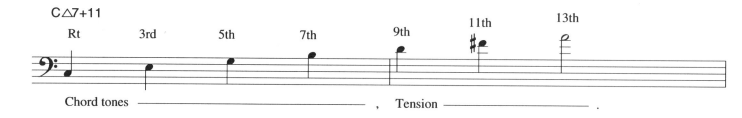

Roots & Fifths
all chord types/various keys

B♭ Blues/Roots Only

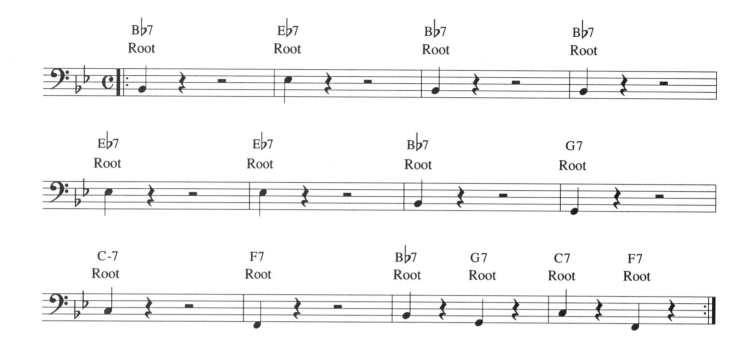

B♭ Blues/Roots and Fifths

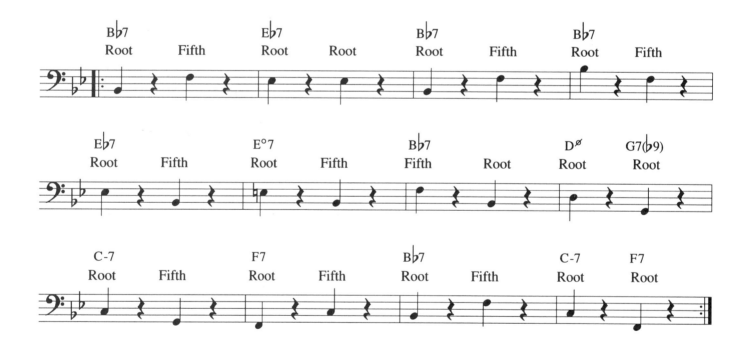

148

Blues

When reading the chord symbols below, play simple basslines in the quarter note rhythm shown. Begin with just roots and fifths in a steady tempo. Later, try to add notes between the roots and fifths, and employ the third of the chords as well. Make sure to play the roots on the down beats (1).

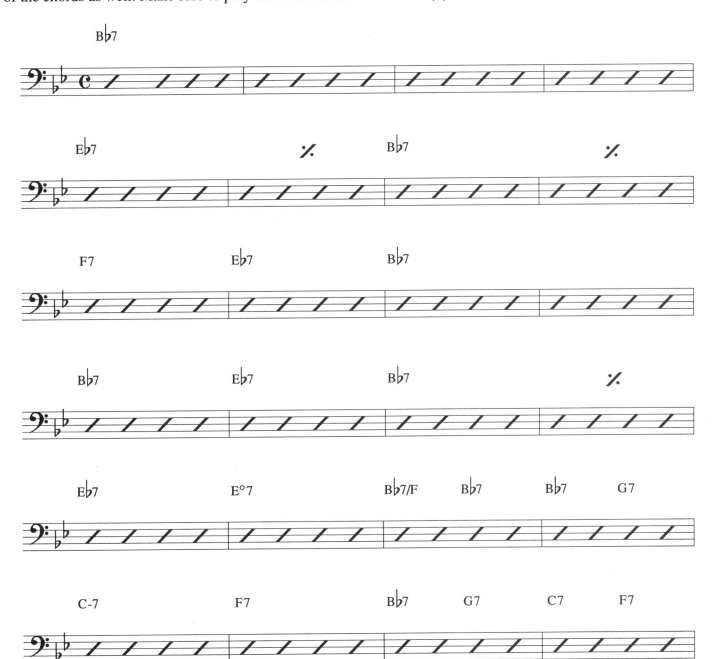

149

Reading Basic Chord Charts

Begin with the root on the downbeat of each chord using the fifth in between (see written notes.) "Walk" means play quarter notes with a bounce and even stride. "Simile" means play similar to what came before.

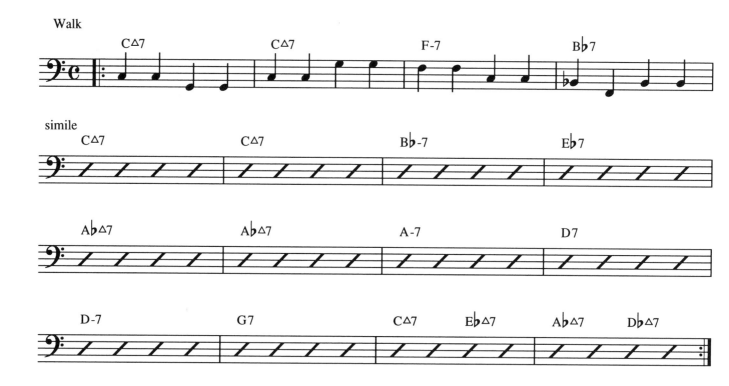

A "Two feel" is accomplished by emphasizing the first and third beat of the measure.

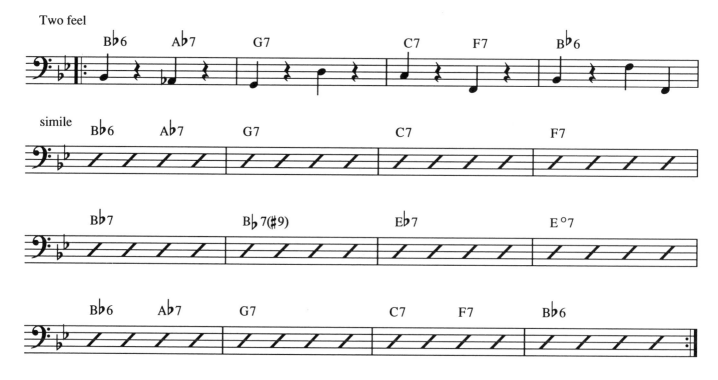

150

Intervals in Position (Upright Bass)

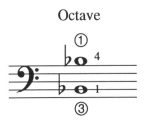

Octave

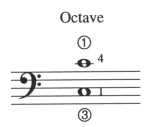

Octave

Roots, Fifths and Octaves

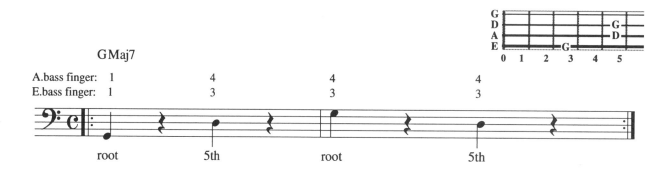

GMaj7

| A.bass finger: | 1 | 4 | 4 | 4 |
| E.bass finger: | 1 | 3 | 3 | 3 |

root   5th   root   5th

Root, 5th, octave bass lines are one of the most common ways of laying down the foundation of the harmony. It is easily playable across three strings in the same position. When rhythmisized these bass lines work in all styles of music. The following bass part is used in many styles in different tempos, (experiment!)

CD 2
Track #11

GMaj   Gmin

Soul beat

B♭min   B♭Maj   Fsus4   F7

waltz

FMaj7

CD 2
Track #12

Walk

Dmin   Cmin   Dmin   Cmin

152

A Minor Bossa Nova/Roots and Fifths

6/8 Latin/Roots, Fifths and Octaves

Grooves/Vamps with Roots and Fifths

Invent your own root-fifth grooves and vamps. Experiment with space and different rhythms. Try using different time signatures.

110 SCALES/MODES
216 CHORD ARPEGGIOS IN 1ST POSITION

The following exercises are for technique and ear training. Listen to the color of each chord as you play the scale/arpeggio. Try playing the examples twice as fast like track 32 or half speed like track 36. Play different rhythms up and down the scales/arpeggios. You may also try improvising over the chords. Experiment with bass lines and melodies. Upright and fretless bassists should match pitch and rhythm with the recording to improve intonation and time.

Major Scales in 1st Position/Bass Guitar

A= Acoustic Bass
E= Electric Bass

158

*This page has been
left blank to avoid
awkward page turns*

Minor Scales in 1st Position/Bass Guitar

Upright bassists will need to shift occassionally between the first 2 positions. (see < or >)

F Melodic minor, ascending

Bb Melodic, minor ascending

F# Melodic minor, ascending

B Melodic minor, ascending

G Melodic minor, ascending

G# Melodic minor, ascending

Ab Melodic minor, ascending

Other scales and modes in 1st position, bass guitar (E)

F Symetric diminished

E Symetric diminished

A Symetric diminished

Bb Symetric diminished

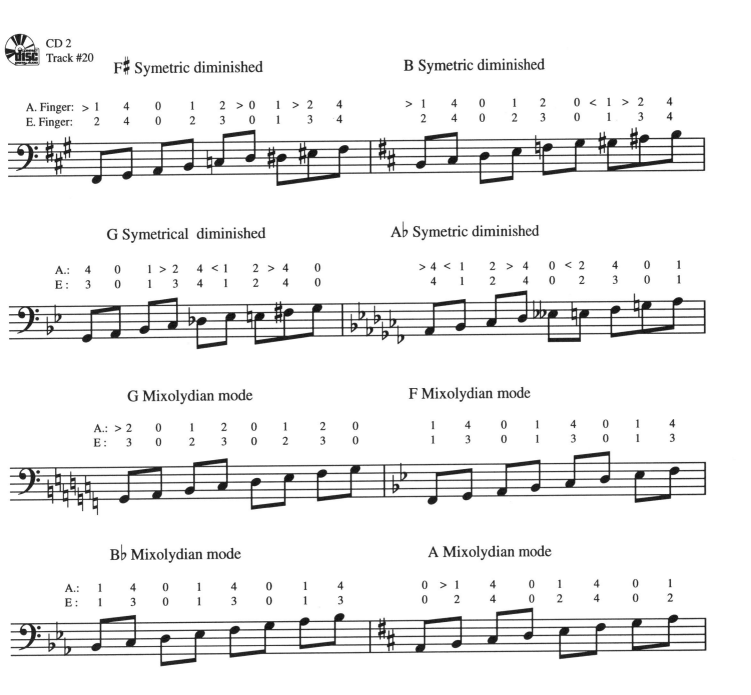

F♯ Symetric diminished

B Symetric diminished

G Symetrical diminished

A♭ Symetric diminished

G Mixolydian mode

F Mixolydian mode

B♭ Mixolydian mode

A Mixolydian mode

Check Points for good intonation (fretless). Listen to the intervals and correct pitch if needed.

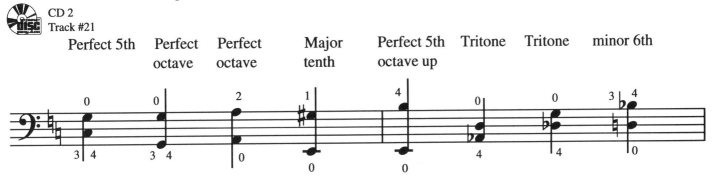

Perfect 5th | Perfect octave | Perfect octave | Major tenth | Perfect 5th octave up | Tritone | Tritone | minor 6th

163

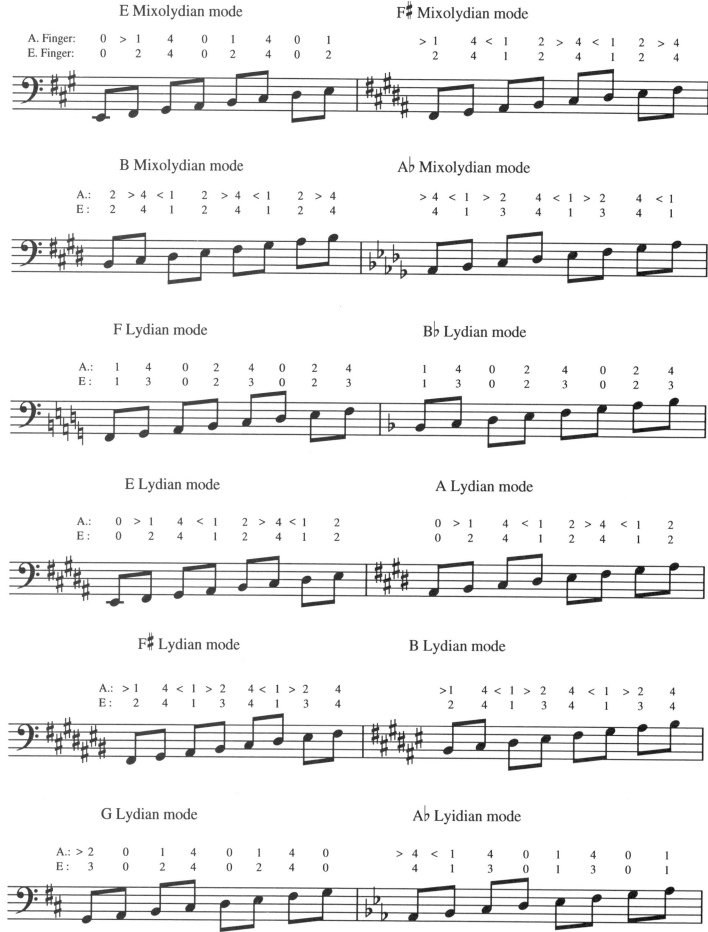

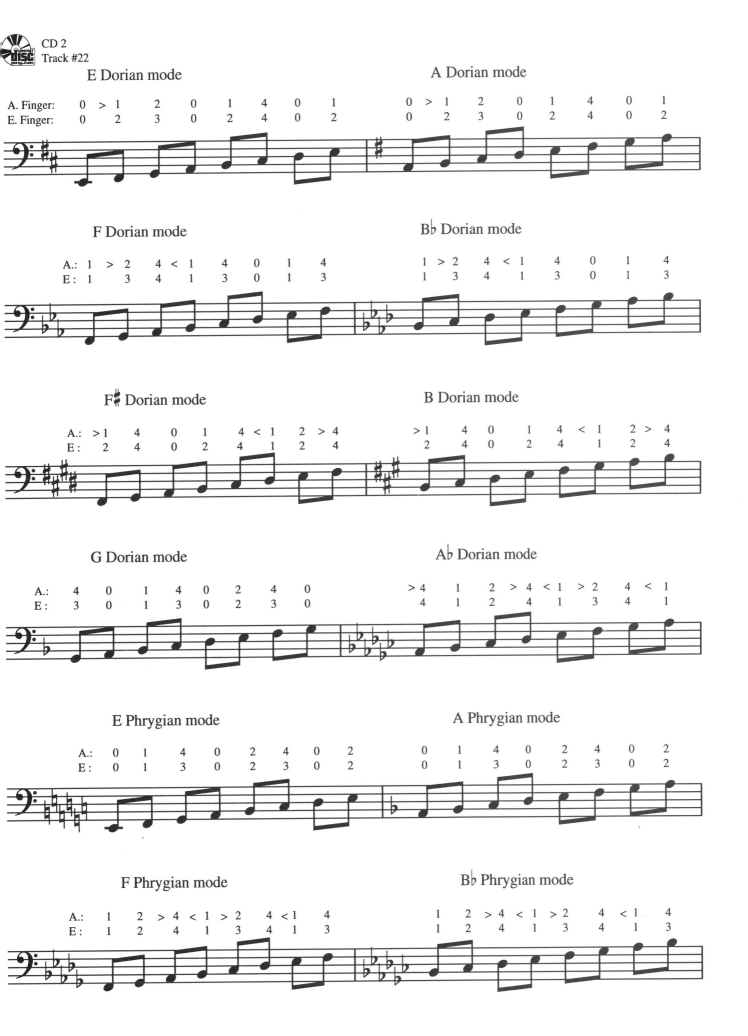

165

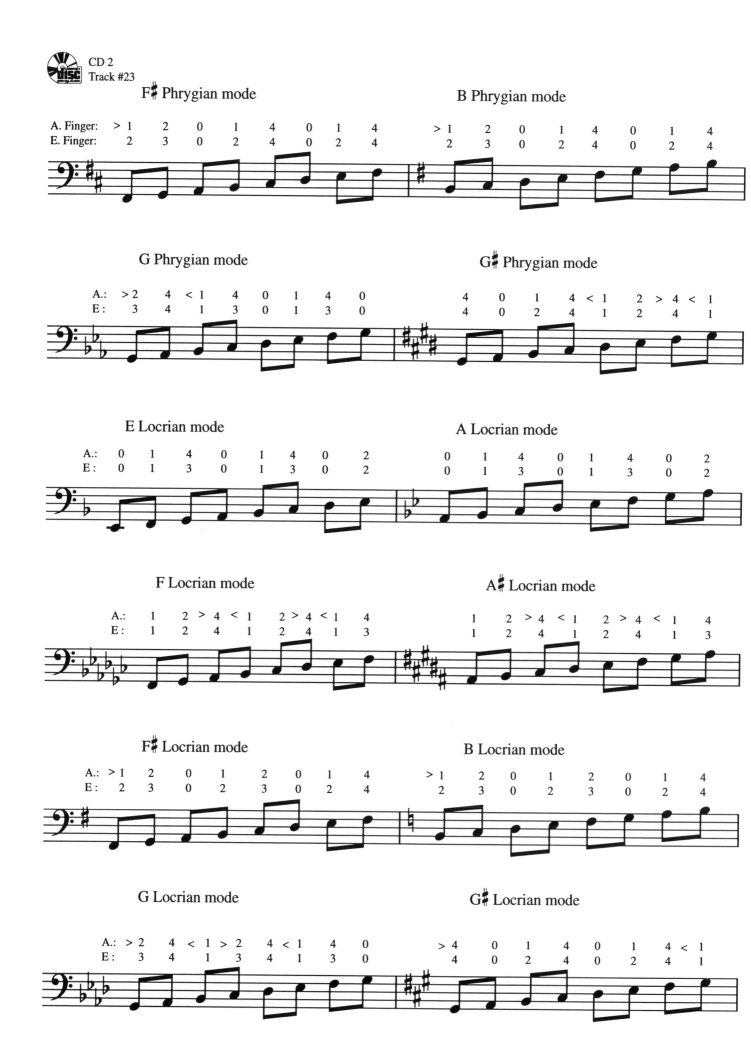

167

Many other scales derived from the Melodic and Harmonic minor scales are also available in this position. See the modes of the minor scales.

First Position Chord Arpeggios From Open E

CD 2
Track #25

Experiment with more possibilities

First Position Chord Arpeggios From 1st Fret F

CD 2
Track #26

Experiment with more possibilities

First Position Chord Arpeggios From 2nd Fret F#

CD 2
Track #27

Experiment with more possibilities

First Position Chord Arpeggios From 3rd Fret G

CD 2
Track #28

Experiment with more possibilities

First Position Chord Arpeggios From 4th Fret A♭

CD 2
Track #29

Experiment with more possibilities

First Position Chord Arpeggios From Open A

Experiment with more possibilities

First Position Chord Arpeggios From 1st Fret B♭

CD 2
Track #31 & 32

Experiment with more possibilities

First Position Chord Arpeggios From 2nd Fret B

CD 2
Track #33

Experiment with more possibilities

First Position Chord Arpeggios From 3rd Fret C

CD 2
Track #34

Experiment with more possibilities

First Position Chord Arpeggios From 4th Fret C#

Experiment with more possibilities

First Position Chord Arpeggios From Open D

Experiment with more possibilities

First Position Chord Arpeggios From 1st Fret E♭

CD 2
Track #37

Experiment with more possibilities